The Eucharist
in the Primitive Church

Prentice-Hall International, Inc., *London*
Prentice-Hall of Australia, Pty., Ltd., *Sydney*
Prentice-Hall of Canada, Ltd., *Toronto*
Prentice-Hall of India (Private) Ltd., *New Delhi*
Prentice-Hall of Japan, Inc., *Tokyo*

The Eucharist
in the Primitive Church

EDWARD J. KILMARTIN, S.J.

Professor
Pontifical Theological Faculty
Weston College

Associate Professor of Theology
Boston College

PRENTICE-HALL, INC.
ENGLEWOOD CLIFFS, N.J.

Imprimi Potest:	John V. O'Connor, S.J. Provincial, Province of New England
Nihil Obstat:	John Walsh, S.J. Diocesan Censor
Imprimatur:	✠ Richard Cardinal Cushing Archbishop of Boston May 28, 1964

To My Mother and Father

This book is concerned with the eucharistic doctrine and practice in the first century. The section which deals with the eucharistic liturgy contains material derived from a later age. However where such references occur, they are only marginal notes.

The sources for the period under consideration are not very extensive. They are confined almost exclusively to the *New Testament* and the brief description of the liturgical service in the *Didache*, chapter 14. There may be, in addition, a connection between the eucharistic liturgy and the liturgical prayers recorded in the *Didache*, chapters 9-10 and *The First Epistle of St. Clement*, chapters 59-61. For the most part, the important *New Testament* texts will be discussed at some length, whereas other references will be treated only incidentally, or not at all. This book is not intended to be an exhaustive examination of the *New Testament* witness to the Eucharist, but rather to serve the interested reader as a point of departure for further study.

Since the scope of this work is so restricted, it cannot be expected to present a complete treatment of the doctrine of the Eucharist as we know it today. It does not take into account the Church's subsequent reflection on the various aspects of this *mystery of faith*. In short, since this undertaking will consider the *New Testament* sources only from a literary and historical point of view, less will be said than is actually contained in this doctrine which addresses itself primarily to the faith.

The contents of this book are divided into three major sections which consider the Eucharist in the stages of *preparation, revelation-realization* and *re-presentation*. The first section discusses *Old Testament* themes and prophecies and the corresponding non-canonical Jewish tradition which seem to testify that God was preparing His people for the revelation of the Eucharist. The second section deals with the origin and interpretation of the words of institution as well as the Pauline and Johannine reflections on the meaning of the Lord's Supper. The final section takes up the practical question of how the Eucharist was celebrated in the primitive Christian communities. In this part three topics of current interest are treated. There is an outline of the evolution of the external form of the Eucharist, an analysis of the structure and content of the eucharistic prayer which enclosed the words of institution and some remarks about the important place which the eucharistic cup occupied in the liturgical action.

Thus the passage from type to reality, from prophecy to fulfillment is traced through three stages. At the middle point of this development stands the Last Supper which both reveals the fulfillment of types and prophecies and at the same time fulfills the revelation. For the Last Supper is both the revelation and the realization of the "Lord's Supper." The subsequent celebration by the Church will be the Lord's Supper only insofar as it refers back to this center; only insofar as it is the re-presentation of the first celebration which took place in the upper chamber; only insofar as it fulfills the deepest meaning of the invitation of Christ: *"Do this in remembrance of me."*

This book is dependent in great part on the extensive current literature published by continental exegetes and theologians. In order to carry out the obligation of acknowledgment and at the same time to provide the interested reader with references for further study, a list of books and articles, which have been particularly helpful to the author, is included. This bibliography is arranged for the convenience of the reader according to chapter and theme. Whenever an author is referred to in the course of this book, the reference to his particular contribution will be found in the appropriate place in the bibliography.

The author wishes to acknowledge the assistance given him in the preparation of this study by his colleagues of the Weston College faculty. Reverend John J. Collins, S.J., Professor of New Testament and Editor-in-Chief of *New Testament Abstracts*, Reverend Francis X. Lawlor, S.J., Professor of Dogmatics, and Reverend Frederick L. Moriarty, S.J., Professor of Old Testament, were especially generous in undertaking the task of reading the manuscript and offering many helpful suggestions.

E. J. K.

Contents

Foreshadowings of the Eucharist
in the Old Testament and in Jewish Tradition

THE OLD TESTAMENT is made up of many literary works which came into being over a considerable period of time. This block of literature which extends back into the remote history of the Hebrew people is the product of many human authors who depended on material which had been transmitted from generation to generation by word of mouth. Since this literature is, in a true sense, the creation of a social group, it is not surprising to find that it contains almost every known type of literary form: poetry, prose, history, annals, legends, straightforward teaching, and so forth.

Diversity is a hallmark of the Old Testament. Yet there is an inner, unifying factor, a characteristic common to all these books. They were produced under the inspiration of God to recount some aspect of the revelation of the divine plan for the salvation of the world. Sometimes events of the history of salvation which have already taken place are recalled; sometimes a glimpse is given, through prophecy, into the future redemptive activity yet to be unfolded in history.

Those of us who look on the Old Testament as the record of the first stage in the history of salvation do not expect to find in it the complete revelation. But because the Old Testament looks forward to the fulfillment in Christ, because it contains the record of God's activity in preparing Israel for that fulfillment, we naturally expect to discover in it some indications of the essential characteristics of the Messianic age. Since the Eucharist is, as the New Testament shows, an important aspect of the eschatological era inaugurated by

Christ, it would not be surprising if there were some hints, however vague, of this gift which is destined to re-present[1] the redemptive act of Jesus in the midst of the community of the new covenant until the Second Coming.

The prophecy of Malachi, the sacrifice of Melchizedek, the biblical themes of the Messianic Feast, the Heavenly Manna are thought by many to provide allusions to the Eucharist and therefore to serve as a preparation for the revelation of the Last Supper. Although one must be cautious in evaluating the evidence, the legitimacy of this claim can be shown.

THE PROPHECY OF MALACHI (THE BOOK OF MALACHI 1:11)

After the return of the Israelites from the Babylonian captivity, great expectations arose concerning the future of the nation. Under the prodding of Haggai and Zechariah, the rebuilding of the Temple was accomplished and dedicated in 515 B.C. With the resumption of the solemn cultic functions, Juda was able to render due worship to Yahweh. However, when Malachi appeared some fifty years later, no substantial progress had been made in the political and economic spheres. Juda remained a small, insignificant province under foreign domination. Disappointment arose because the prophecies of Isaiah, Jeremiah, and Amos had not been fulfilled. In time this disappointment gave way to doubt about the mercy of Yahweh and His love. What was the value of the covenant? Why had not Yahweh exalted His people? Unable to read the signs of the times correctly, both leaders and people were led toward religious indifference.

---

[1] The word re-present is used in this book to signify that the redemptive activity unfolded in an historical event of the past is rendered present here and now in a sacramental manner of existence. However, when the word is used with respect to Old Testament memorial rites, it should not be interpreted that the historical event itself is somehow present in mysterio, but rather that the saving power of the past event is rendered present. When the word is used with respect to the New Testament memorial rite, the Eucharist, it has an added meaning which is in keeping with the interpretation of the words of institution of the Eucharist given in Chapter Two. In the eucharistic celebration there is question of the presence of Christ, the High Priest, who brings to the midst of the Church the same identical offering of obedience and love which He made at the climax of His earthly life.

In this climate of uncertainty, Malachi delivered his prophecy in the name of Yahweh. First, he recalled to Israel Yahweh's love which had so recently been manifested in their regard. Yahweh abandoned Esau and the Edomites and allowed them to be subjugated in the Arab invasion of the first half of the fifth century, B.C., but He protected Israel. However, although Yahweh allowed the suppression of Juda's traditional enemy and saved His own people, the question nevertheless remains: Why has He not fulfilled His promises made through the prophets? According to Malachi, it is because the cancer of religious cynicism has infected the priests of Yahweh. They show by their conduct that they do not appreciate the value of the sacrifices made in the Temple. They offer imperfect gifts, a violation of the Mosaic Law (Deut. 15:21; Lev. 3:1, 6), and Yahweh will not accept them. Malachi thus reveals the rejection of the Levitical cult, but he inserts a ray of hope in announcing a new sacrifice which will be acceptable: "For from the rising of the sun to its setting my name is great among the nations, and in every place incense is offered to my name and a pure offering" (v. 11).

The prophet is emphatic in foretelling the abolition of the Levitical cult: "I have no pleasure in you, saith the Lord of hosts: and I will not receive a gift from your hands" (v. 10). Inasmuch as Yahweh will not accept this sacrifice, it is worthless. In its place a new sacrifice will be substituted, a totally different kind of offering not bound by the law of unity of sanctuary. It is unlikely that the prophet had in mind a form of worship existing at that time either among the pagans or Jews of the diaspora. The characteristics of this new sacrifice, its purity and universality, make it improbable that he was thinking of any sacrificial practice then in use. Some have argued that Malachi refers to a metaphorical sacrifice, a sacrifice in the wide sense such as prayers, a purely internal cult. This interpretation is hardly justified in the context which speaks of ritual sacrifice.

The prophet is speaking of external sacrificial cult, but the type of sacrifice is not indicated. "Incense" or "sacrifice of incense" is a generic term. The word "offering" (minchâh) also has a generic meaning. Some authors have attempted to limit its significance to grain sacrifices, but this would be extremely difficult to prove. In Leviticus 2:1 the word minchâh refers to grain offerings, but in

Genesis 4:4 and Malachi 1:13 it refers to sacrifice in blood. Generally speaking, before the Exile *minchâh* applied to all sacrifices—just as did the word *qorbān*—and after the Exile it was commonly used for unbloody sacrifices. Nevertheless, since it was not exclusively restricted to this type, the generic sense ought to be maintained in this pericope.

If Malachi does not reveal the exact type of sacrifice which is to replace the old form, he does indicate that it has characteristics which relate it to the Messianic era. It is to be universal, both by reason of place and time ("from the rising of the sun to its setting") and people ("among the nations, and in every place"). Such a sacrifice does not fall within the scope of the Mosaic Law, as sacrifice in this context was offered only in Jerusalem (Deut. 12:1-16). Moreover, according to the Mosaic Law the Gentiles were barred from taking part in the sacrifice of Yahweh (Lev. 20:24; Deut. 7:1; Ex. 34:12). This new sacrifice pertains rather to the Messianic age when cult will have a universal character (Micah 4:1-11; Zech. 8:20; Isa. 2:2).

Consequently, Malachi announces a new, true, and proper sacrifice which will belong to the people of the Messianic age. In a vague way he looks forward to the sacrifice of the cross and its ritual representation, the Eucharist, which in the full light of the New Testament revelation appears as the fulfillment of this prophecy. It is interesting to note that the relationship of Malachi 1:11 to the Eucharist did not escape the author of the *Didache*. This document, possibly written before the Fourth Gospel and in any case most probably before the end of the first century, contains one of the first written references to the Eucharist outside the New Testament. Chapter Fourteen mentions the eucharistic celebration which takes place on the Lord's Day and links it to the prophecy of Malachi.

THE SACRIFICE OF MELCHIZEDEK

Psalms 110:4 reads: "The Lord has sworn, and he will not repent: 'Thou art a priest forever according to the order of Melchizedek.'" These words were first addressed to David, but David is seen as the embodiment of the kingdom of Israel and its hope for the future in which the kingship of Yahweh will be extended to all nations. In this sense the psalm is Messianic, for it gives expression to the Messianic character of the Davidic dynasty. The New Testament removes any doubt about the Messianic import of the psalm by explicitly relating it to Christ (Heb. 5:6; 7:17, 21; see also Mark 12:35-37; Luke 22:41-42). But in what sense is Christ a priest according to the order of Melchizedek? Do the references to Melchizedek as a type of the Messiah indicate that Christ is antitype insofar as He instituted the Eucharist?

In Hebrews 7:1-3 a number of reasons are advanced to explain how Melchizedek is a type of Christ. His name signifies "king of justice." He was king of Salem, that is, king of peace. He was without father or mother or genealogy, and thus is likened to Christ who is a priest forever. No mention is made of the type of sacrifice which Melchizedek offered as priest, and so no comparison is made between it and the sacrifice of the cross or the Eucharist. The Epistle to the Hebrews simply does not envision any such comparison, although it does compare in great detail the sacrifices of the Old Law and the sacrifice of Christ. If the author of the Epistle had known of a sacrifice of Melchizedek, it would be rather surprising if he omitted it, since a dominant theme of the Epistle is the notion of sacrifice.

One cannot argue that the author of the Epistle to the Hebrews does not take into account Genesis 14:18 which, according to many modern exegetes, following the interpretation of many Fathers of the Church, speaks of Melchizedek's sacrifice in bread and wine. This could hardly be the case since Hebrews 7:1-3 uses three elements found in Genesis 14:18-20 to show the superiority of Christ's priesthood over that of Aaron. It would seem that the author of this epistle is simply unaware of any sacrificial meaning in the words "brought forth bread and wine."

Although many Fathers of the Church see in the bread and wine mentioned in Genesis 14:18 a type of the Eucharist, and at times refer explicitly to Melchizedek's sacrifice in bread and wine as a foreshadowing of the eucharistic sacrifice, this cannot be taken as proof that Melchizedek actually offered a sacrifice in bread and wine. Nor does the argument advanced by some commentators that the choice of bread and wine at the Last Supper was a deliberate allusion to the gesture of Melchizedek have any real weight. Christ used bread and wine because He was instituting a solemn cultic banquet, and wine was thus called for. To the Hebrews, wine stamped a meal as solemn or festive. As will be seen, fermented drink was characteristic of a solemn cultic meal in the Old Testament (Deut. 14:26), and the description of the Messianic Banquet in Song of Solomon 5:1 and Isaiah 25:6 (55:1-3; 65:11) mentions the use of wine.

The strong probability remains that Melchizedek simply brought forth bread and wine as nourishment for Abraham and his companions. It is very likely that we know nothing of "a sacrifice of Melchizedek." But even if the "bringing forth of the bread and wine" mentioned in Genesis 14:18 originally had no cultic significance, it can be taken as a type of the paternal solicitude of Christ the High Priest, who provides spiritual food for His followers. In this sense Genesis 14:18 could be said to prefigure the Eucharist.

THE MESSIANIC FEAST

A number of factors, under the divine impulse, contributed to the development of the concept of the Messianic Feast. (1) In the Yahwistic recital of the conclusion of the Sinaitic covenant, reference is made to a sacred banquet taken by Moses, Aaron, Nadab, Abihu, and seventy of the ancients of Israel in the presence of Yahweh (Ex. 24:9-11). (2) During the wandering in the desert, Yahweh fed His people and quenched their thirst in a marvelous manner. (3) Numerous references are found in the Old Testament which testify to the strong Israelite tradition of taking sacred meals in the place of sacrifice (Gen. 31:54; Ex. 18:12; 1 Sam. 9:12-14; Hos. 8:13; Am. 2:8).

In all these cases, the taking of food symbolizes Israel's union with Yahweh, especially in the case of the sacred meals taken in the sanctuary. For this reason, great importance is attached to them (Deut. 12:7; 14:23; 15:20), and the solemnity of the occasion is emphasized by the taking of fermented drink (Deut. 14:26). As the Israelite saw it, Yahweh who inhabits the Temple receives at His table those who have come to render homage to Him. This gesture, concretized by the actual eating of part of the victim which had been sacrificed to Yahweh, symbolized the union between the God of the covenant and His people.

Once the importance of the sacred banquets as a religious expression of Israel's union with Yahweh is recognized, one can easily understand how a sacred meal came to be linked with the Messianic expectations. With the development of the Messianic hope, there arose the idea of an eschatological banquet which would unite Israel around the Messiah.

The prominent part played by the Messianic Feast in the scope of the Jewish Messianic expectations is witnessed by a number of Old Testament texts which describe the blessings of the Messianic age in terms of a banquet of which the ritual feast of the Law was a figure. Psalm 22:26 speaks of the Messianic Banquet which will be shared by rich and poor alike, and in Psalm 23:5 we read of the banquet which the shepherd will serve. The Book of Isaiah depicts the happiness of the Messianic age as a banquet (Isa. 25:6; 55:1-3; 65:11-14), and the Song of Solomon appears to refer to the Messianic Feast. If it is an allegory using the language of human love to sing of the ideal union between Yahweh and His people, a union more hoped for than realized, it is likely that Song of Solomon 5:1 refers to the Messianic Feast. Just as the banquet mentioned in Isaiah 25:6, it takes place on the "mountain of incense" mentioned in Song of Solomon 4:6, namely, the site of the Temple. Moreover, this mountain is located in the garden, that is, Paradise, the place *par excellence* of the divine presence. The wine and milk mentioned in Song of Solomon 5:1 are associated with water and wheat referred to in Isaiah's invitation to the Messianic Feast (55:1-3). These foods, opposed as they are to deceptive satisfaction, have a metaphorical meaning. They designate the material and spiritual joy of the Messianic age promised to those who hear Yahweh.

The Feast of Wisdom described in Proverbs 9:5 is a variant of the Messianic Feast and is the most ancient biblical text dedicated to this theme. According to the allegory set forth in Proverbs 9:1-6, Wisdom, just as Yahweh, has her house where she offers a sacred meal. The metaphorical temple is the collection of proverbs for which Proverbs 1-9 serves as an introduction. One can say that

Wisdom herself has constructed this sanctuary since she has formed
the wiseman whose maxims have been preserved in the Book of
Proverbs. The food of the feast is the maxims, and by them man is
nourished as by a divine food. They afford a participation in the
wisdom of Yahweh.

It is clear that this allegory is related to the Messianic Feast because the vocabulary resembles the description of the Messianic
Feast described in Isaiah 65:11-14 and the literary form is similar
to Isaiah 55:1-3. An important difference, however, exists between
the Messianic Feast described in Isaiah and the Feast of Wisdom.
The prophecies look forward to a future banquet, whereas Proverbs
sees the promised feast actualized in some way in the present. According to Proverbs 9:1ff. the faithful disciples of Wisdom have, up
to a point, access to the eschatological goods which the prophets
described by the image of a banquet.

This interpretation of the Book of Proverbs is understandable.
The author is writing in a period shortly after the Exile when the
Davidic dynasty no longer exists and in which the Messianic hope
was related to Yahweh Himself. The author of Proverbs attempts
to show that Divine Wisdom, without being the Messiah, fulfills
the function of the Messiah. She can do this since she possesses qualities inherent to her nature which Isaiah extolled as divine gifts
made to the Messiah.

The Feast of Wisdom is also mentioned in Ecclesiasticus 24:19-21
in a passage which is dependent on Proverbs 8-9. From it we gather
that to be nourished by Wisdom and to hear her word are the same
thing. In Ecclesiasticus 15:3 it was already stated that Divine Wisdom nourishes man with the "bread of understanding" and gives
to drink the "water of wisdom." In this connection Ecclesiasticus
51:13-16, 23-26 adds the appeal of one who has been filled with the
gifts of Wisdom. The wiseman invites others to come and hear
Divine Wisdom with words which are inspired by the Messianic
Feast of Isaiah 55:1-3.

The concept of the Messianic Feast is also found in noncanonical
Jewish literature. The Fourth Book of Esdras 8:52 refers to the
abundance of food prepared for the age to come. The Book of Enoch
62:14 also indicates an acquaintance with the eschatological ban-

quet: "The Lord of Spirits will dwell with them and they will eat with this Son of Man; they will take their places at His table forever and ever."

Finally, the first century Qumran community attests to current Jewish belief in the Messianic Feast. In a recently discovered fragment of the *Rule of the Congregation,* a Dead Sea Scroll of Cave I, there is a description of a meal as it will be celebrated in the Messianic period under the guidance of the priestly Messiah. The procedure to be followed parallels closely the description of the daily meals taken at Qumran and described in the sect's *Manual of Discipline.* Because of this similarity, it has been conjectured that the daily meals of Qumran had for the participants the function of an anticipated Messianic Banquet. This is quite possible and has given rise to the theory that the cultic meals of Qumran lie at the origin of the eucharistic celebrations of the early Church. However, while there are some likenesses, the number of differences will not allow us to speak of a direct dependence of one on the other. There is no evidence, for example, that the meals of Qumran were in any sense a commemoration of the Teacher of Righteousness and still less that they symbolized a relationship to Him or His redemptive work. There is, in fact, no real evidence that the Qumran meals were more than the kind of meals which were common among Jewish religious groups and which must have been observed by early Christians. They should not be confused with a sacramental meal such as the eucharistic celebration depicted in 1 Corinthians 11:17-34.

Having reviewed the texts of the Old Testament and noncanonical Jewish literature, we can summarize the characteristics of the Messianic Feast.

1. *It has the setting of a liturgical meal.* In Isaiah 25:6 it takes place on the mountain, a reference to the mount of Sion where Yahweh dwells (Ezek. 28:14).

2. *It is described as a nuptial meal.* In Song of Solomon 5:1 it is represented as a feast of espousal to which the spouse invites his friends. This image gives to the Messianic Feast the character of a covenant and indicates that it is the occasion for an

encounter of the most intimate sort between Yahweh and the eschatological community.

3. *It is linked with the Son of Man.* In the apocalyptic literature, the Messianic Feast is conceived as taking place not only in the presence of Yahweh but with the Messiah (Enoch 62:14).

4. *It has a transcendent quality.* It surpasses the liturgical banquets of the Old Law which are only types. It takes place in Paradise (Song of Sol. 5:1); it boasts of the abundance of Paradise. Both the quality and superfluity of the food indicates that it takes place in a transformed world (Isa. 25:6; 55:1) and that the blessings derived are spiritual ones (Isa. 55:3).

5. *It is universal in extent.* It is destined for all people (Isa. 25:6).

Turning to the New Testament, we find that the blessings of the eschatological kingdom are described in terms of a banquet (Luke 13:29; 14:15-24) and even a wedding feast (Matt. 22:1-14; 25:10). At the Last Supper Christ's prophetic words, often referred to as the "vow of abstinence," place the Messianic Feast in the context of an eschatological Paschal meal (Luke 22:16-18, 29-30; Mark 14:25; Matt. 26:29). Finally, in the Apocalypse of John, both the nuptial and Paschal themes are associated with the Messianic Feast. The future kingdom is described as the wedding feast of the Lamb (Apoc. 19:9).

But the New Testament does not present the Messianic Feast as something reserved only for the future. To some extent it is realized even during the life of Jesus. The symbolical character of the meals of the Gospels has been commented on by a number of modern authors. Although the Evangelists present Jesus as the master who teaches, He is also shown as one who wishes to unite men around Himself in the social intimacy of a meal which has Messianic significance. The banquets attended by Jesus display a characteristic Messianic joy. Jesus uses this fact to show the contrast between the period of John the Baptist and His own. The former was a time of waiting and fasting; the latter is one of joy and banqueting (Mark 2:18-19; Matt. 9:14-15; Luke 7:33-34). This joy is a sign that the new era has arrived, the time of the Messiah.

Some of the banquets attended by Jesus are clearly meant to symbolize the characteristic goal of the Messianic Feast: union with
God. It is typical of Jesus to eat with publicans and sinners (Luke
7:33-34; 15:2), which shocked the righteous Pharisees who asked on
one occasion: "Why does your master eat with publicans and sinners?" (Matt. 9:11). When Jesus heard this question, He answered:
"Those who are well have no need of a physician, but those who are
sick. . . . For I came not to call the righteous, but sinners" (vv. 12-
13). This answer provides the clue to this exceptional practice of
Jesus: in accepting the intimate fellowship with sinners, He shows
that He has come to destroy the barrier between sinful men and
God.

Not only the earthly meals of Christ but also the Eucharist is
presented in the Gospels as the fulfillment of the Messianic Feast.
This will be shown in the next chapter when the Messianic implications of the Last Supper and the relationship of the Last Supper to
the establishment of the Kingdom are treated. For the present it
will be sufficient to discuss an important passage in the Gospel
according to Luke which seems to imply that the fulfillment of the
Messianic Feast takes place in the Eucharist. Luke 13:28-29 appears
to refer to the entrance of the Gentiles into the Church which is
called the "kingdom of God." If this is so then the reference made
to the participation of the Gentiles in the feast of the kingdom
would relate to the Eucharist.

This same teaching is also found in the very next chapter, Luke
14, where Jesus underlines the thought that the solemn earthly
feasts should typify the gathering of all peoples into fellowship with
God. Commenting on the repast which He took with one of the
rulers of the Pharisees, He told the lawyers and Pharisees:

> When you give a dinner or supper, do not invite thy friends, or
> thy brethren, or thy relatives, or thy rich neighbors, lest perhaps
> they also invite thee in return, and a recompence be made to thee.
> But when thou givest a feast, invite the poor, the crippled, the
> lame, the blind; and blessed shalt thou be, because they have nothing
> to repay thee with; for thou shalt be repaid at the resurrection of
> the just (vv. 12-14).

These words caused an immediate reaction. One of those at table
saw in Christ's words a reference to the Messianic Feast which
would be universal in character. He exclaimed: "Blessed is he who
shall feast in the kingdom of God" (v. 15). This led Christ to re-
spond with a parable which echoes the theme of the banquet of
Wisdom found in the Book of Proverbs. Just as Wisdom sent her
servants to invite all those who passed to feast in her house (Prov.
9:3-6), so the Father sends His servants to call those invited to the
feast, and in the end invites everyone that can be found. Thus, in the
parable the universality of the Messianic Feast is stressed, just as in
the case of the banquet of Wisdom. It is likely, too, that in view of
Luke 13:28-29 the Messianic Feast is understood to take place in the
Church, antitype of the house of Wisdom, and that it is identified
with the Eucharist, antitype of the feast of Wisdom.

HEAVENLY MANNA

The sixteenth chapter of the Book of Exodus describes how
Yahweh fed the Israelites in a marvelous fashion. The food which
was given is called "bread from heaven" because it was thought to
have descended from the sky. As *bread,* it served to sustain the
physical life of the people; as *bread from heaven,* it became a type
of a more lofty spiritual food. According to Deuteronomy 8:2-3, the
supreme purpose of the manna was not to sustain the physical life
of the Hebrews but to serve as a sign of a higher good. It was a
means of instructing the people that the word of Yahweh is the
indispensable nourishment. This teaching is repeated in Wisdom
16:20-26. In verse 20 reference is made to "angels' food . . . bread
from heaven, ready to eat, strong in all enjoyment, and suited to
every taste." But in verse 26 the bestowal of food by Yahweh is
seen to have as its goal the instruction of men: ". . . that it is not
the production of the crops that supports men, but that it is your
word that preserves those who believe in you." This passage, evi-
dently inspired by Deuteronomy 8:2-3, adds a new note, namely,
that the new life conserved by the word is more than a simple
earthly life. It is the eternal life promised to believers in the early
part of the book. This is shown from the fact that the author sup-

presses the "not by bread *alone* does man live" (Deut. 8:3). It is the word *alone* which conserves the believer.

The description of the word of Yahweh as a spiritual nourishment which is superior to material food is found elsewhere in the Old Testament. In general, it is related to all that is said of the sovereign efficacy of the word of Yahweh (Am. 8:11; Jer. 15:16; Ps. 119:103; Ezek. 3:3). The same concept is found in the New Testament and in a text which is inspired by Deuteronomy 8:2-3. When the devil tempts Jesus in the desert to change stones into bread, he answers by quoting the text of Deuteronomy 8:3: "Man shall not live by bread alone, but by every word that proceeds from the mouth of God" (Matt. 4:4). In the Fourth Gospel the same idea is expressed in Jesus' assertion that His food is to do the will of the Father (John 4:34), and especially in the discourse on the "bread of life" (John 6:26-47). This latter pericope harkens back to Deuteronomy 8:2-3 in that it presents manna as a type of spiritual nourishment (vv. 32-33); it is related to Wisdom 16:26 in that it distinguishes a different species of life which is preserved by this spiritual food. Manna, just as all natural nourishment, preserves only mortal life, and that for a time (vv. 27, 49, 59). But the spiritual food, of which manna is a type, gives eternal life (vv. 27, 40, 47). But what is this spiritual food? It is, first of all, the word which Jesus preaches (vv. 35-47), the word of God extolled as *the* true nourishment in the Old Testament. In this respect the discourse of Jesus echoes the teaching of the Book of Deuteronomy, namely, that manna is a sign of the superior food of the word of God, and the tradition of the Book of Wisdom, namely, that the word of God gives a life which is superior to natural life. Going beyond this, however, Jesus introduces a new theme. The manna is not only a type of the word of God, but of the Incarnate Word of God in His eucharistic presence (vv. 54-59). This point will be discussed at length in Chapter Four. We may note also, in passing, that in 1 Corinthians 10:3 manna is called spiritual food. In the context of this pericope, which will be discussed in Chapter Three, it is clear that Paul understands that it is a type of things to come and is fulfilled in the Eucharist.

Manna is an apt symbol or type of the Eucharist because of the

analogy between natural and supernatural *nourishment.* It was
also well chosen by Jesus and the early Church in view of the marvelous way in which it is given: it is a pure gift of God, given
without man's help and in abundance. The only question that
remains is this: Are there any indications in Jewish literature that
a new type of manna, different from the word of God, was expected
in the Messianic era? Do we find in the Old Testament the prophetic
announcement of a new and superior manna, which is distinguished
from the word of God and which also preserves spiritual life? The
answer is in the negative. In certain Old Testament passages, the
manna of the desert was conceived as having marvelous qualities.
It was given the name "bread of the strong" (Ps. 78:25), which the
LXX correctly translates as "bread of angels." The same name
"bread of angels" or "nourishment of angels" is used in Wisdom
16:20 and is carried over into apocalyptic literature outside the
inspired writings (4 Esd. 1:19). Since in late Judaism, angels were
not thought to have need of food (Tob. 12:19), the term does not,
in all probability, refer to the actual nourishment of angels. It has
been conjectured that the phrase should be understood as "the
nourishment borne by angels" acting as intermediaries between God
and man. However it seems more probable that this description of
manna refers to the qualities of the food itself. This is indicated in
Wisdom 16:20 which refers to the "angels' food [manna]" as "strong
in all enjoyment and suited to every taste." Moreover, this explanation is preferred by the Midrash on Psalm 78:25. There it is stated
that manna is called angels' food because it makes the children of
Israel "mighty as angels." Following the same line of thought, the
Babylonian Yoma 75a states that manna was pearl white "because
it makes white the sins of Israel." Nevertheless neither in the Old
Testament nor in the noncanonical Jewish literature do we find the
manna of the desert taken as a type of a superior manna, distinguished from the word of God, which will be the food of the Messianic Kingdom.

In the noncanonical Jewish literature, on the other hand, the
manna of the desert, the very manna which fed the wandering
people, is associated with the Messianic Kingdom. The *Syriac
Apocalypse of Baruch* states: "It shall come to pass at that self-same

time that the treasury of manna shall again descend from on high, and they will eat of it in those years (that is, the period of the temporary Messianic Kingdom on earth), because these are they who have come to the consummation of time." According to the *Christian Sibylline Oracles*, manna will serve as nourishment for the members of the Messianic Kingdom (8:148-149). In the Midrash on Ruth 2:4 we may read: "At the end God reveals himself over you and makes manna descend on you." Rabbinic tradition often pictures Moses as a type of the Messiah insofar as he nourished men with manna. The Midrash on Ecclesiastes 1:9 testifies to this: "As it was with the first liberator [Moses], so it will be with the last liberator [Messiah]. . . . As the first liberator made manna descend . . . so also will the last liberator make manna descend." In the Midrash on the Song of Solomon 2:9 and the Midrash on Numbers (Rabbah) 11 the Messiah is said to cause manna to descend from heaven.

Many other references could be given to show that Jewish tradition associates manna with the Messiah. It will suffice to mention one more. Commenting on the significance of Joshua 5:10-12, which reports that manna fell for the last time during the night of the fourteenth of Nisan, rabbinic sources teach that the remaining manna is stored in the heavenly world against the day of the appearance of the Messiah which will occur in the month of Nisan. This manna is depicted as the food of mankind in the world to come and as continuing to be made in special mills in the third heaven. Of special importance is the link which is placed between the Messiah, manna, and the Passover. The reappearance of manna will coincide with the appearance of the Messiah at the time of the Passover. It will be the sign by which the Messiah is known.

When we turn to the New Testament, we find confirmation of the existence of Jewish beliefs or speculations about manna. In John 6:15, after the miraculous multiplication of the loaves and fishes, it is stated that the crowd wished to make Jesus king. This reaction provides indirect evidence for the current Jewish belief about the eschatological manna. The crowd seems to have recognized in this prodigy a sign of the manna of the Messianic age and thus identifies Jesus with the Messiah. They see the miracle as a manifestation of the prophet like Moses announced in Deuteronomy 18:15, and so cry out: "This is indeed the prophet who is to come into the world" (v. 14).

However, on the next day when the rush of enthusiasm has subsided, it becomes clear to the crowd, at least to those engaged in conversation with Jesus, that the bread of the feeding miracle was not the bread of the Messianic age. They do not consider it a sufficient sign to prove that Jesus is the Messiah. It is a gift inferior to the manna which Moses had procured (vv. 30-31). If Jesus wishes to prove that He is the Messiah, He must perform a miracle comparable to that of Moses, perhaps even give the manna of the Messianic age. The underlying presupposition of this dialogue is the intimate relationship between the manna of the desert and the epiphany of the Messiah.

There is clear evidence from the noncanonical Jewish literature and the New Testament for the popular belief in the eschatological significance of the manna of the desert. But there is an important difference in the way in which the significance of manna is understood. In Jewish speculation, the manna of the Messianic Kingdom is identified with the manna of the desert. The New Testament writers, however, understand the manna of the desert only as a type of divine blessing reserved for the Messianic age. In John 6:26-47 it is portrayed as a type of the word of God, and in John 6:54-59 and 1 Corinthians 10:3 as a type of the Eucharist.

SACRIFICIAL BLOOD

This chapter, concerning the foreshadowings of the Eucharist, would not be complete if we did not discuss the question of whether or not the Old Testament considers the sacrificial blood of the Old Law as a type to be fulfilled in the Messianic age.

It will be recalled that sacrificial blood is a sacred "gift" offered to a deity in a theistic culture. The ritual action involving blood implies the presence of a living being whose blood is offered as a symbolic expression of basic religious attitudes. Through this rite, man renders visible his interior act of adoration of the author of all life. He may use it as a means of externalizing his thanksgiving for benefits received or to express his intercession for new favors or as a dramatic confession of his need for forgiveness when he has sinned. The Israelites, just as their neighbors, held blood in high regard. It was considered to be the principle of life in some vague way (Lev. 17:14); it was almost identified with life itself (Deut. 12:23). Among the Israelites, moreover, it was reserved for Yahweh alone, the author of all life. Its use was restricted to worship.

Before the covenant of Mt. Sinai (Ex. 24:8), sacrificial blood was offered by the heads of families. Afterwards, when the Levitical priesthood was established, it was ordinarily and officially offered by this class of society. In the sacrificial ritual, blood was splashed around the altar and on special occasions sprinkled on the people (Ex. 24:8) or on the priests (Lev. 8:23; Ex. 29:20).

In almost all types of sacrifice in which blood was offered, the sacrifice of the Paschal lambs being an exception, an expiatory or atoning element was prominent. In Leviticus 17:11 Yahweh indicates that sacrificial blood is an acceptable ritual sign by which man may acknowledge that he really deserves God's punishment for sins. If offered with the proper dispositions it will serve as the occasion for atonement. Purification and divine pardon will follow; in consequence of which, Israelites will be able to approach the tabernacle of Yahweh with a good conscience.

In the Old Testament there are no explicit references to the "new covenant" blood which will fulfill the function played by sacrificial blood in the Old Law. The sacrificial blood of the Old Law is not portrayed as a type to be fulfilled in the eschatological kingdom, but the concept is implicit in the revelation of the role of the 'Ebed Yahweh. Although human sacrifices were strictly forbidden for the Jews of the Old Law (Deut. 12:31; 18:10; Lev. 18:21), nevertheless the task of the 'Ebed Yahweh, the Servant of Yahweh, was approved by Yahweh Himself. Through the activity of the Servant, Yahweh promises to establish a covenant with all the nations (Isa. 42:6; 49:6, 8). The Suffering Servant will make satisfaction for the sins of others (Isa. 53:4-6). He will present himself as a guilt offering ('asham: Isa. 53:10). In brief, his death will be expiatory, and the value of his offering is stressed in Isaiah 53:11. The sacrifice of the old covenant emerges, therefore, as a type of the eschatological covenant which Yahweh will establish through the *'Ebed Yahweh*. It prefigures the new covenant announced by Isaiah and Jeremiah (Jer. 31:31-34). Because, according to the Hebrew outlook, a covenant is made only with blood (Gen. 15:9-18; Ex. 24:4-8)—without the shedding of blood there is no covenant (Heb. 9:15-22)—the "new covenant" concept implicitly contains the idea of sacrificial blood. Thus, the sacrificial blood of the Old Law can be shown to have a typical meaning for the new covenant.

The New Testament reveals that Christ is the *'Ebed Yahweh*. His blood is the "blood of the new covenant." The interpretation of the blood of the dying Christ as sacrificial, as the fulfillment of the Mosaic type, is emphasized in the Mark and Matthew accounts of the institution of the Eucharist, as will be seen. It is stressed in the Epistle to the Hebrews, where the old covenant is shown to be a type of the new and superior covenant which Christ the High Priest inaugurates "by His own blood" (Heb. 9:11-12). His blood is a sin-offering so superior to the sacrificial blood of the Old Law (Heb. 9:13-14) that it cannot be offered again (Heb. 9:11-12). Once and for all it effects a profound atonement which renders the old covenant sacrifices obsolete (Heb. 10:1-10).

The theme of the saving power of Christ's blood runs throughout the New Testament. St. Paul speaks of it in his preaching (Acts 20:28) and in his letters (Rom. 3:25; Eph. 1:7; 2:13; Col. 1:20). The same concept is found in 1 Pet. 1:2, 19 and in John 6:54-59; 19:34; 1 John 1:7. Nor is the Apocalypse lacking in testimony to the salutary effects of Christ's blood (Apoc. 1:5; 5:9; 7:14; 12:11; 19:13).

From what we have seen, we can conclude that the New Testament depicts the fulfillment of the implicit Old Testament vision of a superior sacrificial blood which seals the new covenant. However the New Testament goes beyond even the implicit revelation of the Old Testament in that the latter contains not the slightest allusion to the ritual of drinking blood at the Messianic Banquet. Although the new covenant, a new and superior covenant blood, and the Messianic Banquet lie within the scope of the Old Testament eschatological hope, there is not the slightest hint that the sacrificial blood of the new covenant will be the drink of the eschatological banquet of the Kingdom. Indeed, the very concept would be, a priori, repugnant to the Hebrews who were forbidden by Divine Law from drinking any blood under pain of death (Gen. 9:4; Lev. 17:10-14). Hence, on this point Christ transcends the Old Testament type and prophecy for He reveals that the wine associated with the Messianic Banquet in the Old Testament (Song of Sol. 5:1; Isa. 25:6; 55:1; 65:11) is His blood. He invites His followers to drink His blood in the banquet of the Kingdom; a drinking which the primitive Church extolled as efficacious for the development of the spiritual life of the individual and the community as a whole. It effects, together with the heavenly manna of the new order, the union of each believer with Christ and the other members of the Church (1 Cor. 10:16-17). It causes, according to the testimony of the Fourth Gospel, a reciprocal indwelling between Christ and the believer, life everlasting, and the resurrection of the body in glory (John 6:54-59).

CONCLUSION

Our study of the foreshadowings of the Eucharist in the Old Testament leads us to the following conclusions:

1. The prophecy of Malachi looks forward to the Messianic age in which a new form of worship, universal in character, will be offered to God. In a vague way the prophet announces the Eucharist which alone, in the full light of revelation, fulfills the details of the prophecy. Hence Malachi contributes to the understanding of the sacrificial character of the Eucharist.

2. The sacrifice of Melchizedek remains problematic. Perhaps the most we can say is that the historical action of Melchizedek is a type of Christ's eucharistic gift insofar as he exercises paternal solicitude in offering food to Abraham and his followers.

3. The Messianic Feast of the age to come is announced in the Old Testament and in the noncanonical Jewish literature. Since the New Testament attests that the Feast finds its fulfillment in the Lord's Supper, the Eucharist must have been thought by the primitive Church to possess the characteristics

of the traditional description of the Messianic Banquet. This means that the Eucharist was understood as a joyful, liturgical meal which involves an encounter between God and the community through the Messiah and a sharing in the abundant, transcendent blessings of the Messianic age.

4. The manna of the desert, a gratuitous gift of Yahweh, is depicted in the Old Testament as being marvelous in its own right. It is the "bread of angels" in the sense that it is a superior nourishment which gives the Israelites great strength. It is also a type of spiritual food, the word of God, which preserves the spiritual life. In the noncanonical Jewish literature, the ability to effect a cleansing from sins is attributed to it. Furthermore it has an eschatological significance: it will be an ingredient of the Messianic age, given by the Messiah at the time of the Passover which will inaugurate the new era. In the New Testament, the Jewish traditional teaching regarding manna is gathered and sifted. The popular belief that the manna of the desert will be enjoyed in the Messianic age is rejected, but manna still retains an eschatological significance; it is a type of the Eucharist. This affirmation of the primitive Church sheds light on her understanding of the Eucharist. As antitype of the nourishment which afforded the Israelites marvelous strength, the Eucharist must be a superior food, comparable to the word of Yahweh which is antitype of the manna according to the Old Testament tradition: a spiritual food which preserves supernatural life.

5. The sacrificial blood of the Old Law is a type of the sacrificial blood of the New Law. Hence, the effects attributed to the former must, in a higher degree, be predicated of the latter. Although the Old and New Testaments affirm this fact, the Old Testament does not allude to a sacramental participation in the sacrificial blood of the New Law. Nevertheless, when the redemptive significance of the sacramental participation in the sacrificial blood of the New Law is revealed, the meaning attributed to sacrificial blood in the Old Law throws light on the meaning of participation in the sacramental blood of Christ. To communicate in the blood of Christ means for the

believer a deeper involvement in the new covenant with all that this entails for the individual's personal destiny, his relation to the community of the covenant, the Church, and the great mass of humanity which, while outside the visible Church, nevertheless radically and essentially falls within the scope of the redemptive work of Christ and therefore within the covenant.

The Words of Institution

PRELIMINARY OBSERVATIONS

THE NUMEROUS EXPLICIT and implicit references to the Eucharist in the New Testament are directly traceable to the words of institution. It would seem that the one public revelation of the Eucharist took place at the Last Supper. Although many scholars believe that the promise of the Eucharist, mentioned in John 6:54-59, is an independent revelation, there are supporting reasons for the opinion that the author of the Fourth Gospel employed the account of the Last Supper in this pericope in order to make explicit what Christ implied in the historical "bread of life" discourse. (The basis for this opinion will be discussed in Chapter Four.) Even the so-called private revelation which many exegetes believe was made to Paul, on the basis of 1 Corinthians 11:23, has been seriously questioned. Today scholars prefer to interpret Paul's words as a reference to the exalted Lord who instructs through the Church. Consequently, they understand Paul to be speaking of a revelation which Christ gave at the Last Supper and which the Church preserves in her teaching.

Since the revelation made at the Last Supper is most probably the unique historical source of the Church's knowledge of the Eucharist, the subsequent teaching of the Church concerning this sacrament is derived from this source alone. Reflecting on the words and gestures of Christ, with the help of the Holy Spirit, the Church came to recognize all the eucharistic dogmas which she has set forth as articles of faith. The words of institution should not be thought of as a ray of light which illumines the eucharistic dogmas. Rather, the dogmas are rays of light originating from the revelation given at the Last Supper. Distinguished from one another by the reflective activity of the Church, they can be turned back on the source and can serve as means of further enlightenment.

Because of the importance of the words of institution for the understanding of the Eucharist, we shall begin our study with a detailed consideration of the accounts of this revelation which are found in the three Synoptic Gospels and the First Epistle to the Corinthians. However, by way of introduction, it will be advantageous to consider a common characteristic of many modern interpretations of the institutional accounts. This discussion will enlighten us regarding the task of a modern study of the texts and at the same time help to explain our method of procedure.

When we look through the maze of explanations of the origin and meaning of the accounts of institution which have come to light during the last seventy or eighty years, we find that they range through a spectrum in which every conceivable possibility has its advocates. However there is one point on which many influential scholars are agreed, though at first glance they may appear to have almost nothing in common—that is, a willingness to admit that in apostolic times the Eucharist was understood as a *sacrificial meal.* This is the opinion of Rudolf Bultmann and Hans Lietzmann, but the latter adds that another type of Eucharist also manifested itself in the primitive Church: a joyful meal orientated toward the Second Coming of Christ. Both these authors are in agreement about the origin of the Eucharist, that neither type was instituted by Christ. At the other end of the pole stands Joachim Jeremias who holds that the Eucharist, during the first century, was understood as an eschatological meal and that it was instituted at the Passover feast by Christ. Jeremias rejects the hypothesis of a sacramental meal allegedly introduced into the Church by St. Paul.

Although Lietzmann and Bultmann may seem to have nothing in common with Jeremias, they all argue from the same basic presupposition which to a great extent finally decides the question of the origin and/or meaning of the Lord's Supper: the refusal to accept the possibility of the dominical institution of a sacrificial meal.

This can be shown from a more detailed comparison of the opinions of Bultmann and Jeremias, which represent the two extremes in the modern study of the Eucharist.

For Bultmann the original meaning of the Eucharist was sacramental, although he attributes the accounts of institution to the Hellenistic Church. In other words, we are concerned here with an etiological cult legend originating in a Hellenistic milieu. According to this legend, a sacramental meal is given the character of an institution derived from Christ. The Synoptic accounts of the institution of the Eucharist at the Passover are mere historizations of a legend which grew from the developing tradition on which the Synoptics depended. In this interpretation, the presupposition that a sacramental meal could not have originated in a Palestinian milieu, much less from Jesus, decides the conclusion regarding the *origin* of the institutional accounts.

Jeremias, unlike Bultmann, does not begin with a sacramental understanding of the Eucharist but with an historical and linguistic study of the pertinent Gospel passages. He concludes that Mark 14:22-24 stems from a Palestinian milieu and that this account contains, in substance, words spoken by Jesus at the Paschal meal. But he will not admit that Jesus instituted a sacramental meal. The only alternative for Jeremias is to find in Jesus' words and actions at the Last Supper a twofold parable which must be interpreted in the framework of the Passover. The broken bread becomes a parable of the fate of Jesus' body and the wine, the blood of the grapes, a parable of His outpoured blood. The subsequent giving of the bread and wine to the Apostles indicates that they will have a share in the redemptive effect of Jesus' death. Hence Jesus' command: "Do this in remembrance of me," does not refer to a sacramental meal; rather it manifests His desire that the Apostles should continue their daily meals together, praying God to remember His Messiah and bring the consummation to pass. As Jeremias understands it, the Lord's Supper was an eschatological meal in the primitive Church.

Jeremias is guided by the same basic presupposition as Bultmann: the impossibility of the dominical institution of a sacrificial meal. Only in this case the assumption influences the *interpretation* of the words of institution. Bultmann, because he interpreted the words of institution as referring to a sacrificial meal, denied that they originated with Jesus. Jeremias, on the other hand, having shown to his satisfaction that the institutional accounts substantially contain the words of Jesus spoken at a Paschal meal, denies that they are sacramental in tenor. Both Bultmann and Jeremias assume as certain that Jesus could not have instituted a sacramental-sacrificial meal.

But why are Bultmann, Jeremias and Lietzmann, among others, so opposed to the concept of the dominical institution of a sacramental-sacrificial meal? Many reasons are advanced by these authors, but it is sufficient to note here that quite frequently the opposition appears to be based on the belief that sacramental realism has no place in the economy of salvation preached by Jesus. This presupposition, however, cannot be taken as a first principle. It demands proof, especially since we are dealing with a redemptive economy in which *the Word became flesh and dwelt among us.*

In any case, clearly contradictory views of eminent scholars cannot all be correct. Bultmann's theory that the Eucharist is a sacramental meal originating in the Hellenistic Church cannot be reconciled with Jeremias' thesis that the Eucharist is an eschatological meal instituted by Jesus at the Last Supper. Lietzmann's conclusion that there were two types of Eucharist in the primitive Church is not compatible with the position expressed by Oscar Cullmann, namely, that there was one Eucharist which included both characteristics.

Confronted with this situation, the task of modern studies of the Eucharist is clear. To evaluate these several theories concerning the origin and meaning of the Eucharist, it is altogether necessary that one begin with the study of the text and context of the words of institution in the light of modern historical and literary criticism. In keeping with this program, this introduction to the study of the institutional accounts will consider (1) problems regarding the text: sources, literary character and comparative age of the accounts; (2) the context of the words of institution in the Gospel narratives; (3) an interpretation of the accounts of institution which is based on the foregoing data and the meaning of the words themselves in a first-century Palestinian context. Support for our conclusions will be found in the following chapters which treat essential aspects of the Pauline and Johannine theology of the Eucharist.

THE TEXT

Sources

There are five accounts of the Last Supper recorded in the New Testament (Matt. 26:17-30; Mark 14:12-26; Luke 22:7-38; John 13-17; 1 Cor. 11:23-25). Only four mention the institution of the Eucharist. The Fourth Gospel which devotes a good deal of space to the events of the Last Supper omits this information. The reason for this omission will be discussed in Chapter Four. We will leave for the present a consideration of this problem and concentrate on the accounts of institution and the special difficulty associated with the fact that they are not identical.

LONG AND SHORT VERSIONS OF LUKE   Although the four accounts mention the Eucharist, it was commonly held during the early part of this century that only three accounts, in their original forms, agreed on essentials. Luke 22:19b-20 was considered a late addition which should not be attributed to the Evangelist. This account of the institution was thought to end with the words: "And he took bread and gave thanks and broke it, and gave it to them, saying, 'This is My body' " (v. 19a). Luke was supposed to have testified to an anomalous order in which the eucharistic cup (vv. 15-18) preceded the eucharistic bread. To bolster their position, advocates of this theory pointed out that important manuscript witnesses leave out verses 19b-20. But since the overwhelming weight of manuscript authority favors the longer text, modern critics are more inclined to accept the longer text as the original and the shorter one as a mutilation. Such a mutilation would be understandable in a post-apostolic community which recognized the eucharistic coloring associated with the cup of verses 17-18 and wished to avoid having two eucharistic cups in the one account.

SIMILARITIES AND DIFFERENCES IN FOUR ACCOUNTS   Since Luke
22:19-20 appears to be genuine, we have four accounts which are
substantially in agreement but nevertheless show some noteworthy
differences. Agreement on essentials indicates that the accounts are
derived from the same basic source. Differences of expression betray
later special influences.

The first thing one notices when comparing the four accounts,
after their common traits, is the similarities which exist between
Matthew and Mark and between Luke and Paul. This observation
gave rise to the terms *Fons Petrinus* and *Fons Paulinus*. It was generally thought that Matthew and Mark reflected a primitive Palestinian tradition associated with Peter and that Luke and Paul
handed on a Hellenistic tradition associated with Paul. The obvious
verbal differences which set these groups apart—there is also a
theological outlook which will be discussed later—are indicated in
the following schema.

	FONS PETRINUS	FONS PAULINUS
Words spoken over bread.	Only the words: "This is My body."	Body characterized as "which for you" (Paul); "which is given for you" (Luke).
Words spoken over wine.	Blood directly related to the covenant.	Blood related to the covenant through the term *cup*.
	Blood characterized as "which is shed for many."	Blood characterized as "which is shed for you" (Luke).
	Expiatory effect of blood mentioned in Matthew: "in remission of sins."	
Order of procedure.	No indication of time of the blessing of the wine.	Wine blessed "after the meal."
Actions of Christ.	Christ blessed, broke, and gave bread to disciples.	Luke mentions same action but Paul omits reference to giving of bread.

	FONS PETRINUS	FONS PAULINUS
	Christ took, blessed, and gave cup to disciples.	This action implicit in words: "in like manner also the cup."
Invitation of Christ to Apostles.	Christ invites Apostles to eat and drink (Matt.); to eat (Mark).	Luke and Paul omit mention of invitation to eat and drink.
	No invitation to repeat the rite.	Paul and Luke record invitation to repeat rite over bread.
		Paul mentions the invitation to repeat rite over wine "as often as you drink."
Actions of Apostles.	Mark observes that all drank of the cup.	No mention of any action by Apostles.

RELATIONSHIP OF DEPENDENCE   The substantial agreement among the accounts of institution indicates, as we have said, that they derive from one source. Until recently many exegetes—following on the heels of Lietzmann, Bultmann, and others who had refined earlier attempts along the same line—maintained that the unique source was the Hellenistic Church which transformed the Last Supper and the subsequent fraternal meals of the earliest Christian communities into a sacramental meal reminiscent of a mystic rite of Greek origin. However, scholarly research, especially during the last thirty years, has established a Semitic background for all the elements of the words of institution. Because of this evidence, there is, at present, a more general readiness to admit that a Palestinian source lies behind the four accounts and even to accept the Last Supper as that source. In order to explain the differences among the accounts, a number of influences are assigned, both liturgical and cultural.

Modern scholars commonly agree that Mark presents a Palestinian version which is expanded by Matthew. The relationship between Luke and Paul is disputed. Some believe that there is a direct relationship. Pierre Benoit, O.P., for example, argues that Luke makes use of Paul and Mark. Others, such as Jeremias, treat Paul and

Luke as representatives of different traditions: Paul is linked to the Hellenistic Church and Luke is related to a Syrian milieu. In his recent study of the institutional words in Luke, Heinz Schürmann has given evidence for the existence of an ancient, nonliturgical source of which Luke seems to be the oldest and most accurate rendition; Paul is judged to have made use of the same source and to have expanded it for instruction.

Perhaps the most we can say on this question is that although Paul and Luke have many similarities, they also have many differences, and the source of Luke may well be other than Paul and vice versa. On the other hand, they both may have depended on the same basic tradition. Whatever may be said of the mutual dependence of the accounts on one another and their immediate sources, however, it is evident that they are all linked with the actual celebration of the Lord's Supper in the Christian communities of the primitive Church. The *Sitz im Leben* of the accounts of institution is the primitive liturgy. The accounts are not formulations made up by the Synoptic writers or St. Paul to serve as a report of what happened at the Last Supper.

Literary Character

Modern authors have good grounds for stressing the liturgical character of the institutional accounts. The context of the Pauline narrative found in 1 Corinthians 11:23-25 indicates that this formula was used in the cultic meal of the Corinthian Church. Paul recalls it as something well known to the Corinthian Church, something which they associated with the actual celebration of the "Lord's Supper" (1 Cor. 11:20). The institutional account found in Mark shows signs of having existed as a unit independent of the Passion narrative and so offers another clue to the liturgical character of this pericope. In Mark 14:18 the introduction to the Paschal meal proceedings begins with the phrase: "And while they were eating. . . ." Again in verse 22, which serves as the introduction to the words of institution, the same phrase is employed. This repetition is not in keeping with the relatively smooth style of Mark and indicates that what follows is not completely at home in the present setting. In other words, the institutional account stands out as relatively independent of the pericope in which it is found. Hence, the distinct possibility arises that this passage was taken over from the liturgy of the primitive Church and incorporated in the Markan passion narrative. Beyond all this, however, there are strong reasons for maintaining the liturgical character of the words of institution drawn from a consideration of the accounts themselves. Both the manner of presentation and the literary style indicate that the original narrative was, in the course of time (a short time at that), "liturgized."

PRESENTATION   All the accounts of the actual institution of the Eucharist lack historical details which one might ordinarily expect of a writer who is narrating an important event. How unlike these accounts is the Fourth Gospel's description of the washing of the feet (John 13:1-20). No allusion is made to the festive meal procedure although the context appears to be a Paschal meal (Matt. 26:17ff.; Mark 14:12-16; Luke 22:7-18), or at least a festive meal with a Passover coloring. In all the accounts, the unessential details of the meal are placed in the background; all information which is not necessary for a knowledge of the factors involved in the ritual celebration of the Eucharist is omitted. This mode of presentation is best explained on the supposition that the texts, as handed down to us, are the actual accounts used in the liturgical celebration of the Lord's Supper, wherein the primitive Church kept only the remembrance of the essential actions of Christ which were required in order to carry out the re-presentation of the essence of the Last Supper.

LITERARY STYLE   In all the accounts a paralleling tendency is evident, which is characteristic of liturgical prayers. In Luke the parallel construction between the words spoken over the bread and wine is more evident than in Paul although the Markan formula shows still more symmetry, the account of Matthew indicates the most advanced stage of development along these lines.

In view of this evidence, we are justified in considering the institutional accounts as liturgical formulas used by the primitive Church when repeating the Lord's Supper. It is worthy of note, however, that the acceptance of this conclusion does not involve a denial of the historical value of the accounts. To say that a text has been "liturgized" does not mean that it has lost its value as an historical report. It simply describes the precise way in which the Church transmitted the account of the historical event which took place at the Last Supper. The early Church consciously looked on the Eucharist as an *anamnēsis*—a commemoration of what Jesus said and did at the Last Supper—and so preserved in its eucharistic banquet, in a form consistent with a liturgical action, the words and actions of Jesus which were essential for the commemoration.

PAUL'S CLAIM TO A SPECIAL REVELATION   An apparent difficulty arises in asserting that Paul's account is a piece of strictly formulated ritual tradition which he received from the actual eucharistic liturgy. Does not Paul claim: "For I received from the Lord, what I also delivered to you . . ." (1 Cor. 11:23)?

Although at first glance it might appear that Paul is referring to a direct revelation, the liturgical style and presentation of the historical account of the institution of the Eucharist as well as the fact that the account contains idioms foreign to Pauline usage argue against this conclusion. As we have already remarked, more commonly today scholars agree that Paul is alluding to the exalted Lord who works through the Church. Paul received the tradition from the primitive community of Christians, but sees the exalted Lord as operative in the transmission of this tradition.

Comparative Age of the Accounts of Institution

Granting that the four accounts are liturgical in character, we may now turn to the question of their comparative ages. Which is the oldest account? Which lies closest to the Last Supper and hence reflects more faithfully the actual words of Jesus?

Scholars agree that 1 Corinthians 11:23-25, recorded in A.D. 57, is the oldest written account. But we cannot argue from this fact that, absolutely speaking, it is the oldest version. Like the other three, it existed in the oral tradition before being written down. Paul gave it to the Corinthians in A.D. 51, when conducting his second missionary journey, but he received it much earlier. It is probable that he encountered it at Damascus (Acts 9:10-21) or dur-

ing his subsequent visit to Jerusalem when he met the Apostles
(Acts 9:26-27) in A.D. 36-38. At the very latest, his knowledge of the
account would have been obtained at Antioch in A.D. 40 (Acts 11:25).
Although this is a very early account, it is not necessarily an older
text than that of Luke or Mark/Matthew, which also existed at a
very early period in the liturgy of the Church. The question becomes: Which is the oldest *oral* tradition?

Some scholars believe that the age of the accounts can be deter-
mined by the number of Semitic expressions they contain. On this
basis, following the analysis of J. Jeremias, Mark would be the oldest
and Paul the most recent. However the number of "Semitisms" is no
certain measure of the age of the account. The presupposition that
the number of Semitisms would be drastically reduced through the
constant use of the institutional account in a Hellenistic milieu is
undermined by the fact that the Pauline formulation, written about
ten years before Luke, has fewer "Semitisms" than Luke. Actually
the number of Semitisms depends on the skill of the translator
rather than on the age of the account, and it could happen that the
oldest Greek version actually contains the least Semitisms.

It has also been argued that one can deduce the oldest formulation from the way in which the various accounts have been introduced into the narrative of the Last Supper. H. Schürmann, for example, has given persuasive arguments which show the strong possibility that the redaction of Luke is older than that of Mark. But
what does this mean for the actual age of the institutional account?
Since the accounts existed as separate units before being introduced
into the narrative of the Last Supper, we cannot judge the age of
the accounts by the age of the redaction.

Finally, it has been proposed that the oldest account must be
that which preserves best the remembrance of the actual course of
the farewell meal which Jesus took with His disciples; or, at least,
shows the least liturgically developed form of the account. Arguing
on this basis, Paul and Luke would seem to be the oldest as they
preserve best the actual course of the farewell meal. The phrase
"after the meal" makes explicit the fact that the blessing of the cup
followed the meal. Moreover the command, "Do this in remembrance of me," is mentioned only by Paul and Luke. This notion of

memorial banquet which had a fixed place in the Paschal feast seems to have been expressed explicitly by Christ in order to contrast the Old and New Pasch and to indicate His desire to have this eucharistic celebration continued. Both these phrases, therefore, indicate the nearness of Paul and Luke to the historical Last Supper. Thus, one might argue that the phrase "after the meal" is omitted by Mark and Matthew because of the natural evolution of liturgical forms to more conciseness of expression. The lack of the command to repeat the rite as a memorial could be explained also on the basis of the laws of liturgical development; that is, the eucharistic celebration, after a certain period of time, became so familiar to Christians that no special mention of the command was deemed necessary. As P. Benoit observes: "One does not recite a rubric, one executes it."

Viewing the evidence, there is good reason for accepting the command of remembrance as an authentic saying of Jesus. The detail concerning the time of the blessing of the cup also seems to stem from an early tradition antedating Mark and Matthew. So in these two aspects Paul and Luke have preserved elements of a tradition that is more detailed and presumably older than Mark and Matthew.

On the basis that the least "liturgized" must be the oldest accounts, one would have to say again that Paul and Luke are the oldest because they show less symmetry and conciseness of expression, the two telltale marks of liturgical influence. It is perfectly understandable that a nonsymmetrical account would become symmetrical through constant liturgical use, but that the symmetry of a liturgical text constantly in use would gradually be destroyed is hardly likely. Arguing from this principle, therefore, the symmetry observable in the words spoken over the bread and cup in Mark and Matthew manifests a later development than the Pauline and Lukan formulations.

FONS PETRINUS	FONS PAULINUS
This is My body.	This is My body which (is given) for you.
This is My blood of the covenant.	This cup is the new covenant in My blood.

The other sure indication of a "liturgized" text is conciseness of expression. We have already seen that Mark and Matthew omit the historical details of the time of the consecration of the cup and the command to repeat the rite, and thus betray a later development which follows the laws of liturgical evolution. The same evolution is observable in the omission of the phrase, "which is given for you." It seems clear that some such phrase would have been used in connection with the blessing of the bread at the Last Supper to indicate the full significance of "body of Christ," since the blessing of the bread was separated from the blessing of the wine by a whole meal. A fitting interpretation is given in the Pauline and Lukan formulations: The body given to the Apostles is the body offered to the Father. However with the evolution of the form of the liturgical celebration of the Eucharist, the consecration of the bread was joined to that of the cup at the end of the meal and the words of institution which Christ had spoken separately over the bread and wine were linked together in one eucharistic prayer. It was now possible to interpret the meaning of body by the meaning attached to the words spoken over the cup. This is done in Mark and Matthew, and in the process the phrase "which (is given) for you" is replaced by "which is shed for many"; the latter phrase is linked with the words of interpretation spoken over the cup. Hence, the omission of the phrase "which (is given) for you" is a good example of liturgical evolution.

We can conclude, on the basis of the laws of evolution toward symmetry and conciseness of expression which govern liturgical formulations, that the Pauline and Lukan accounts are, generally speaking, the most ancient traditions. However, we must not overlook the fact that they too show signs of the effect of liturgical use. There is, for example, the "Graecizing" evident in the phrase "which is given *for you.*" In Mark and Matthew this concept is transferred to the words spoken over the cup, but instead of "for you," the Semitic expression "for many" is used. This latter expression was probably found in the original form of the Pauline and Lukan accounts in connection with the bread. It is likely that the new expression was introduced because the non-Semitic world, where the Pauline and Lukan formulas were used, did not grasp the significance of the original phrase "for many," which means a totality and not a multitude in contrast to the whole. Therefore, in this respect Mark and Matthew preserve a more ancient element than Paul and Luke.

THE ANTIOCH-PALESTINIAN ACCOUNT   From what we have just seen, it would seem fair to say that although both Paul and Luke, and Mark and Matthew, contain elements of an earlier, more primitive institutional account, the oldest available forms are the former. These accounts preserve a greater exactness in the description of the Last Supper and manifest to a lesser degree the effects of liturgical influence than the corresponding Mark and Matthew versions. Paul and Luke are slight variations of a common basic narrative employed most probably in the early community of Antioch, which can be dated around A.D. 40. However, it was not formulated first in Hellenistic Antioch; rather, the Semitic form of expression indicates a Palestinian source. Hence, its origin should be sought in Jerusalem.

If we remove secondary forms found in Paul and Luke, the original Antioch-Palestinian account probably had the following structure:

> And having taken bread, He blessed, broke and gave to them and said, "This is My body which is given for many; do this in remembrance of Me." In like manner also the cup after the meal, saying, "This cup is the new covenant in My blood."

This formulation, reconstructed by Johannes Betz, is based on certain preferences, many of which have been already indicated and which are summarized in the following chart.

TEXT	REASONS FOR PREFERENCE
And having taken bread He blessed,	Luke is supported by Matthew and Mark. Paul changes for stylistic reasons. *Eulogēsas* of Mark and Matthew (which equals to bless) is Semitic. *Eucharistēsas* of Paul and Luke (= to give thanks) shows a Hellenistic influence.

TEXT	REASONS FOR PREFERENCE
broke,	Found in all accounts.
and gave to them	Luke is supported by Mark and Matthew.
and said	Paul is supported by Mark and Matthew.
This is My body	Found in all accounts.
which is given for many;	Luke is correct grammatically, and the phrase is necessary for understanding the meaning of body at the Last Supper where a meal separated the two consecrations. Paul is in poor Aramaic form and was probably shortened by the source on which St. Paul depended. "For many" is preferred to "for you." It is a Semitism preserved in Mark and Matthew in the words recorded over the cup.
do this in remembrance of Me	This is noted by Paul and Luke. It is in keeping with the Passover setting and intention of Jesus.
In like manner also the cup after the meal, saying	This is noted by Paul and Luke. It is in keeping with the form of a Jewish festive meal.
This cup is the new covenant in My blood.	This is noted by both Paul and Luke.

There are two notable omissions in this reconstruction. Luke 22:20 contains the phrase "which is shed for you." It is not found in Paul and is grammatically incorrect in the Greek text. This phrase should refer to the blood, but through the use of the nominative case for "which" actually refers to the cup. It appears to be a late addition which came about through the influence of an account related to Mark and Matthew. The persistence of this incorrect form can be explained on the basis of liturgical use; that is, the oral recitation would allow for such inexactness of expression. Paul's addition, "Do this as often as you drink in remembrance of Me," is also excluded. This sentence may well have derived from Paul himself in view of the remark which immediately follows: "For as often as you eat this bread and drink this cup, you proclaim the death of the Lord, until He comes" (1 Cor. 11:26). However, it should be noted that this addition lends symmetry to the Pauline account in that there are two commands of remembrance. So possibly this addition should be attributed not to Paul but to a previous liturgical influence.

Concerning the Antioch-Palestinian account, one final observation is in order. This account probably does not present all that Christ said over the bread and wine, but instead gives the substance of His words. It offers a short, concise presentation of the institutional account, which reflects the influence of the primitive Church's liturgy, which in turn is concerned only with the essence of the Last Supper, with its meaning for all time.

THE CONTEXT

Before undertaking the interpretation of the words of institution, we must consider the context in which they were spoken. Our discussion will turn on three points: (1) the relationship of the Last Supper to the Paschal meal; (2) the Messianic implications of the Last Supper; (3) the relationship of the Last Supper to the establishment of the Kingdom.

The Relationship of the Last Supper to the Paschal Meal

If Christ intended to institute the Eucharist at the Paschal meal, this fact should be of value in determining the meaning of the Eucharist. Two questions, therefore, present themselves. Was the Last Supper a Paschal meal or in some way linked to the Paschal meal? What is the meaning of the Eucharist in this setting?

WAS THE LAST SUPPER A PASCHAL MEAL? To answer this question we must consider the evidence drawn from the words of institution, the context surrounding these words, and the arguments which militate against a Paschal meal setting.

From the words of institution we learn that the Last Supper was a fraternal meal which followed the order of a Jewish festive meal: (1) the blessing and distribution of bread at the beginning, (2) the meal itself, (3) the solemn blessing over the wine at the conclusion. There is no indication that the Last Supper was a Paschal meal, which in itself does not prove that it was not. We must remember that we are dealing with liturgical formulas, telescoped accounts, which are not concerned with recounting all the historical details of the final meal Jesus took with His disciples before His passion, but only with reporting the words of institution and the essential gestures associated with them.

Going beyond the words of institution, we find that all the Synoptic accounts of the Last Supper indicate that it was a Paschal meal. We are told that the day had arrived for the celebration of the Pasch and that Jesus intended to carry out the prescriptions of the feast (Matt. 26:17; Mark 14:12; Luke 22:8). In the Lukan account, the institution of the Eucharist is situated within the framework of the Paschal meal itself (Luke 22:15-18). Although in the actual words of institution no mention is made of the Passover meal, Luke recalls the desire of Jesus to eat the Pasch with His disciples before He suffers. This information may have been recorded to contrast the Jewish and Christian Paschs: lamb and cup of the Old Law (vv. 15-18); bread and cup of the New Law (vv. 19-20). Furthermore, since there is good evidence that verses 15-18 are an ancient and independent account of the institution of the Eucharist, it is likely that in some areas of the Church mention of the Pasch was made in the very recital of the institutional account. The most telling arguments for the eucharistic character of verses 15-18 are the following: (1) The cup mentioned in verse 17 appears to be the third cup, the "cup of blessing" (1 Cor. 10:16) which comes after the meal. As leader, Jesus would bless the third cup, whereas in all probability the other cups would be blessed by the participants themselves. This appears to have been the common procedure in the first century. (2) The phrase "He gave thanks" (*eucharistēsas*) of verse 17 describes the act of blessing with a technical eucharistic term. (3) The phrase "Take this" (*labete*) of verse 17 is liturgical terminology associated with the accounts of institution found in Mark and Matthew. (4) This first cup corresponds to the eucharistic cup of Mark 14:25, for both cups are associated with a vow of abstinence. (5) Finally, the invitation to share the cup is unusual—foreign to Jewish table usage—and is best

explained on the basis that Jesus granted leave to the Apostles to
drink. Such a gesture would be required since Jesus Himself did
not drink. The usual sign to begin drinking was the partaking of
the cup by the leader of the banquet.

There is, consequently, some basis for the theory that Luke
22:15-18 draws on a tradition which describes the institution under
the form of the cup. In this description the cup would stand as
pars pro toto for the whole Eucharist, just as in the Acts of the
Apostles 2:42 the "breaking of the bread" stands for the whole
eucharistic celebration which includes the consecration of the wine.
Also, in this formulation, the nexus between the Eucharist and the
Paschal meal would have been explicitly established.

Turning to the circumstances of the actual celebration of the
Last Supper, as described by the Synoptics, one finds some persuasive evidence for the Paschal character of that feast. To show the
points of similarity between the Last Supper and the Paschal meal,
it will be useful to review first the details of the Jewish Paschal meal
and then indicate how the Synoptic description of the Last Supper
fits into this setting.

It is not possible to give an exact description of the first-century
Paschal meal. A cursory glance at a number of reconstructions
reveals many disagreements regarding details. All the descriptions
of the Jewish Paschal meal are based on later rabbinic writings
which do not present a uniform picture and, furthermore, patently
manifest evolved customs which were not current in the first century. The original ritual described in Exodus 12 is rather simple,
but in the course of time many changes were introduced. In the
first century, for example, the Paschal meal was a solemn meal
taken reclining in the style of free men. The Hellenistic practice
replaced the earlier custom of eating the meal standing, with loins
girded, sandals on the feet, and staff in hand, as if ready for a
journey (Ex. 12:11). Of special note in the evolution of the Paschal
feast is the appearance of the prohibition against the Paschal sacrifice being offered outside Jerusalem. This meant that all the lambs
had to be slain in the Temple of Jerusalem and that the Paschal
meal had to be eaten in the Holy City. Two aspects of the original
Passover celebration remained unchanged: (1) the prohibition

against breaking the bones of the lambs and (2) the prescription
that the whole lamb must be eaten.

After the first century, the ritual of the Passover became more
complex. New ritual actions were added, and prayers were amplified. Nevertheless, the most important aspects recorded by later
writers do go back to this period and present the following picture.
It was required that the Paschal feast take place in Jerusalem when
night had fallen and that the participants of the feast spend the
night in Jerusalem. (For the Passover, Gethsemane was included
within the confines of the Holy City.) Shortly after sundown, the
participants of the banquet, at least ten in number, met at the
appointed place within the walls of Jerusalem and took their places
on couches, lying on the left side so that the right hand was free
to be used in eating the meal. The father of the family, or the
leader of the group, probably opened the proceedings with the
blessing for the day, after which he spoke the blessing for the wine.
Whether or not the leader invoked a blessing over the first wine
cup for all the participants is not known with certainty. Whether
or not a common cup was shared by all the participants in the first
century is also a disputed point. In any case, a blessing was recited
over the first wine cup and it was drunk. The right hand was then
washed, and there followed the eating of the hors d'oeuvres, bitter
herbs dipped in vinegar sauce. These were chewed deliberately to
recall the bitter years of captivity in Egypt. Thereafter the Paschal
lamb and the unleavened bread were brought out but not yet eaten.
A second cup of wine was mixed but not yet drunk. At this juncture, at least in later times, the leader recalled the meaning of the
feast and the symbolism of the ingredients of the meal. The bitter
herbs evoked memories of the slavery of Israelites under the Egyp-
tians. The unleavened bread was a reminder of the bread which did
not have time to rise on the night of deliverance. The Paschal lamb
symbolized the lambs slain on that memorable night, the blood of
which was smeared on the door posts of the houses to ward off the
avenging angel of the Lord. The wine was interpreted as a symbol
of joy and gratitude to Yahweh the redeemer. In the first century,
it is probable that the symbolism of each element of the banquet

was explained as it was given to the participants to eat. In later times, after the interpretation of the feast had been given, the first part of the Hallel (Ps. 113 or 113-114) was sung. In the first century, however, the first part of the Hallel was probably sung after the eating of the Paschal lamb.

When the second cup had been drunk, both hands were washed. Then the leader blessed the unleavened bread, broke it, and distributed it to the participants. The Paschal lamb was eaten with the unleavened bread. When the meal was finished, a particularly solemn blessing was said over a third cup by one participant (leader or guest of honor?) for all present. Then either this cup was passed around for all to drink therefrom or wine was poured from this cup into the individual cups. When this had been drunk, the second part of the Hallel (Ps. 114-118 or 115-118) was sung. In later times a fourth cup was mixed and drunk, but it is not certain that this practice was observed in the first century.

A number of details which differentiated this meal from the ordinary festive meal have been pointed out many times. The uniqueness of some of these details has, at times, been exaggerated. For example, it is often stressed that the use of wine indicates a Paschal meal, but as was mentioned previously, wine was characteristic of any festive meal. Authors also have emphasized that the participants of the Paschal meal reclined instead of following the usual custom of sitting. However, this Hellenistic custom was most probably employed in the first century at all festive banquets whenever possible. Nevertheless, there are five details prescribed for the Paschal meal which were unique:

1. The celebration of the Passover took place in Jerusalem when night had fallen, and the participants were required to remain within the defined limits of the Holy City throughout the night.

2. The breaking of the bread took place after the hors d'oeuvres instead of at the very beginning of the meal.

3. The Hallel was sung.

4. The symbolism of the food was explained by the father or leader.

5. The Paschal lamb was eaten.

The Synoptic accounts of the actual proceedings of the Last Supper indicate that the Evangelists place it within the category of a Paschal meal. The celebration took place in Jerusalem, and after the meal Jesus went to the Mount of Olives as if to spend the night there. This action was in accord with the prescription requiring the participants of the Paschal feast to remain within the confines of the Holy City throughout the night. Moreover, Jesus broke bread during the course of the meal, as Mark makes clear, and He interpreted, in a new way to be sure, the meaning of the bread and wine. Finally at the Last Supper the Hallel was sung.

No explicit mention is made of the eating of the Paschal lamb, and the accounts do not state that the meal took place after sundown. Mark and Matthew simply state that they met in the evening, and Luke records that the meal took place "when the hour had come" (22:14). However, the details we possess certainly indicate a Paschal meal setting. If we depended only on the Synoptics, we would have little difficulty in concluding that the Last Supper was a Paschal meal. The objection has often been raised that the sanctity of Friday, the Passover according to the Synoptic tradition, would not be compatible with the fact that the Sanhedrin met, that Simon of Cyrene was returning from the fields, that Christ was executed and buried. However this objection has been met by the research of a number of scholars. At present there is agreement that these details can be harmonized with the prescriptions of the Passover.

The one really serious objection to the identification of the Last Supper with the Passover meal is drawn from the Fourth Gospel. According to John 18:28, the Jews refused to enter the praetorium when they brought Jesus to Pilate "that they might not be defiled, but might eat the Passover." So according to John, the Paschal meal took place on Friday night. Following this method of reckoning, it would be impossible to equate the Last Supper with the Paschal meal. The following chart shows the discrepancy between the Synoptics and John.

NISAN (MARCH-APRIL)	SYNOPTICS	JOHN
13 Wednesday (Synoptics) Thursday (John)		Last Supper
14 Thursday (Synoptics) Friday (John)	Last Supper	Paschal Meal
15 Friday (Synoptics) Saturday (John)	Passover	Passover

Different solutions have been proposed to resolve this apparent contradiction. Some scholars believe that the Synoptics are correct and that John delays the Paschal meal one day for theological reasons. He wishes, it is argued, to have the death of Jesus coincide with the killing of the Paschal lambs in the Temple. This opinion has some merit. It is in accord with John's inclination toward symbolism, and it is in harmony with his description of the crucified Christ as antitype of the Paschal lambs (John 19:36). However, this theory remains only a possibility.

Another group believes that Jesus anticipated the Paschal meal in view of His death which would not allow Him to celebrate it on the Passover eve. At this meal many of the Paschal meal customs were observed, except for the eating of the Paschal lamb which could not be obtained until the following day. Because this meal had the characteristics of the Paschal meal, the Synoptics dated it on the fourteenth of Nisan. Tradition, influenced by the Synoptic presentation, took Jesus' last meal as the normal Paschal meal. This theory, which would make John's dating correct, has some basis in history. There is evidence for a first-century practice of celebrating the Passover by using characteristic Passover rites but not the lamb. This variation would be used by certain pious Jews who were unable to go to Jerusalem. Nevertheless, it cannot be shown that Jesus actually made use of this custom, and again we find ourselves in the realm of pure conjecture.

Other scholars have argued that different ways of calculating the Passover were in vogue during the first century. The Synoptics followed one system of reckoning and John another. According to one rather popular theory, the Synoptics used the Pharisaic calendar and John the Sadducaic. Mlle. Annie Jaubert of the Sorbonne University recently proposed the theory that Christ used an old sacerdotal calendar, which was noted in Book of Jubilees and was actually in use in the first-century community of Qumran. The Synoptics followed this calendar. John, on the other hand, is correct in saying that the chief priests observed the Paschal meal on Friday, for they were following the official calendar which had been in use since the second century B.C. These theories present interesting possibilities, but can scarcely be said to have met with unqualified approval. There is no solid evidence to support the Pharisaic-Sadducaic calendar theory, and it must be said that the proposal of Mlle. Jaubert has not met with sustained enthusiasm. The original wave of interest which arose at the time of her first publication on this subject has subsided.

In view of the evidence at hand, we cannot say that the Last Supper was *certainly* the Paschal meal of that year. Yet it is implied in all the Synoptic accounts that this final repast was taken in the atmosphere of the Paschal feast. Moreover, the words of institution make it evident that Christ intended the Last Supper to coincide with the Paschal meal, at least symbolically, as the occasion for the establishment of the memorial banquet of the new dispensation which would replace that of the Old Law. Just as Yahweh commanded the Israelites to celebrate the Passover as a memorial of His saving work, so now Jesus commands His Apostles to celebrate the Eucharist as the memorial of His saving work: "Do this in remembrance of Me."

Since Jesus used the Old Pasch, or at least the setting of the Passover, as the point of departure for the establishment of the memorial banquet of the New Law, we should place the words and actions of Jesus in the atmosphere of the Jewish Passover feast in order to appreciate their meaning.

The Passover was and remains one of the most solemn feasts of the Jewish year. Concerning its origin, it is not possible to draw any conclusions from the etymology of the name of the feast. An analysis of the feast as described in Exodus 12 reveals that it was made up of two originally independent feasts: (1) the feast of the Passover and (2) the feast of Matzoth. By the time of the composition of Exodus 12, the feasts were united; and they were so closely identified in New Testament times, that one feast was called by the name of the other (Luke 22:1).

The Passover feast, described in Exodus 12:1-14, grew out of a springtime festival sacrifice of a young animal to secure the fecundity and prosperity of the flock. This most ancient pastoral practice was probably in use among the Hebrews in pre-Mosaic times, when they were seminomads. If Exodus 5:1 refers to the Passover ritual, then we have evidence that this ritual was employed before the Exodus.

The feast of Matzoth, mentioned in Exodus 12:15-20, arose from an ancient agricultural feast in which an offering was made of the first fruit of the crop (Lev. 23:9-14). This feast was probably borrowed from the Canaanites when the chosen people had adopted a semisedentary life in the promised land (Lev. 23:10). The word *matzoth* means unleavened bread or unfermented bread and gave its name to the feast (Luke 22:1) since a characteristic of the festival was the prohibition against leavened bread. The feast was observed at the beginning of the barley harvest, which was the first crop to be gathered. It lasted seven days, during which time only bread made from the new grain could be eaten. Since the bread was made without leaven, without anything from the previous harvest in it, it represented a new beginning.

Because of the common features of the two springtime feasts, it was natural that they should be combined in later times. This synthesis is witnessed in the Pentateuch which relates them to the Exodus from Egypt. Under divine inspiration, the feasts of the first fruits of the flock (Passover) and the crop (Matzoth) became the commemoration of the crucial springtime intervention of Yahweh: the deliverance of Israel from the slavery of Egypt.

The profound significance of the Passover feast may be gathered from a consideration of its main characteristics as described in the Old Testament and in rabbinic writings.

It is a liturgical feast, involving sacrifice and an accompanying cultic banquet, celebrated by the community of the chosen people. Accomplished in the present, it commemorates the deliverance from Egypt in such a way that it re-presents the past redemptive activity and looks forward to the future definitive intervention of Yahweh.

It is a liturgical feast involving sacrifice: The killing of the Paschal lambs was considered a sacrificial rite (Deut. 16:1-8). However, the Passover sacrifice was not looked on as an expiatory sacrifice. Because the complete lamb was eaten—none was given to Yahweh—there is a difference between this sacrifice and the ordinary peace sacrifice.

And an accompanying cultic banquet: The Paschal meal was a sacrificial meal because the Paschal lambs were eaten. The elaborate ritual of the meal also indicates its cultic nature.

Celebrated by the community: The social character of the Paschal meal is evident. *All the people* were supposed to participate in this feast *at the same hour, in groups of not less than ten. All the participants* were obliged to *partake of the lamb.*

Of the chosen people: Only the chosen people could participate (Ex. 12:43-49), and the observance was not only a right but a duty (Ex. 12:6; 12:48ff.; Num. 9:13). In ancient times all who were not able to carry out the observance of the Passover at the proper time were required to do so one month later (Num. 9:10-13).

Accomplished in the present, it commemorates the deliverance from Egypt in such a way that it re-presents the past redemptive activity: The observance of the Pasch was not considered a mere subjective remembrance. Rather it was in some mysterious way identified with the historical night of deliverance (Ex. 12:42-43). According to rabbinic teaching, the participants were to keep before their eyes the past redemptive activity of Yahweh, which happens also in the present under symbolical form for their benefit (*Pesachim* X:5).

And looks forward to the future definitive intervention of Yahweh: With the growth of the Messianic consciousness, the hope of the future and definitive intervention of Yahweh was associated with the Paschal feast. Isaiah 11, a Messianic prophecy, was recited on the eighth day of the Paschal feast according to a very ancient tradition. The eschatological note is also struck in the Hallel which was sung at the Paschal meal. Moreover, rabbinic commentators directed the attention of the participants of the Paschal meal toward the future consummation (*Pesachim* X:4-6).

If the Last Supper was not a Paschal meal, it was carried out in the atmosphere of the Passover. Christ intended it to coincide, at least in spirit, with the solemn feast of the Jews. So, according to the intention of Christ, the Eucharist is antitype of the Passover meal, which indicates that there must be some analogy between the two cultic banquets. The significance of the Old Pasch should shed light on the meaning of the Lord's Supper.

The Passover was a memorial re-enactment in symbolic form of the basic event of salvation which took place at the time of the Exodus, the abiding results of which are rendered present through the rite. The New Pasch is also a memorial feast in the Jewish understanding of the term, which Jesus teaches with the words "Do this in remembrance of Me." Even if these words are judged to be an addition of the primitive Church, they express an understanding which ought to be considered as conforming to the mind of Jesus; there is no reason which can be adduced to deny this statement in the name of history. The importance of the memorial aspect of the Last Supper will be discussed later. We need only note here the obvious comparison between the Paschal meal of the Old Law and the Lord's Supper, both looked on as memorial rites. The memorial character of the Paschal meal involved the re-presentation, the reactualization of the redemptive activity of Yahweh manifested at the time of the Exodus, and the consequent sharing in this event by the participants of the feast. The Eucharist, as a memorial celebration, must also involve the re-presentation, the reactualization of the redemptive work of Jesus, for the benefit of the participants of the Lord's Supper.

Moreover, since the Paschal feast was inseparably bound up with the events leading to the Sinaitic covenant, it seems fair to say that a remembrance of that covenant was also included implicitly in the Paschal celebration. J. Jeremias even presents evidence, somewhat fragile when applied to the first century, that the blood of the Paschal lambs was deemed covenant blood just as was the blood of circumcision. In any case, granting the intrinsic relationship between the Pasch and the covenant, the Paschal meal must be recognized as a re-presentation, reactualization, and even reinforcement of the covenant through its effect of revitalizing the bond between Yahweh and the chosen people.

The Last Supper, being the fulfillment of the Old Pasch, should also have a covenant significance; and this significance is testified to by all the accounts of institution. Hence the Lord's Supper, the New Pasch, must in some sense involve the re-presentation, the reactualization, the reinforcement of the new covenant for the benefit of those participating in it. The importance of this aspect of the Eucharist will also be discussed later.

The Messianic Implications of the Last Supper

The Evangelists portray the Last Supper as an important aspect of the Messianic work. The fact that they all give it an important place in the passion narrative is proof enough. Furthermore, in Luke 22:14 the words of Jesus allude to an intimate connection between the Last Supper and the redemptive work: "I have greatly desired to eat this passover with you before I suffer." Perhaps of great significance in this matter is the use which Luke makes of the key Synoptic text identifying Jesus with the Servant of Yahweh. In Mark 10:45 (Matt. 20:28), Jesus says: ". . . for the Son of Man also has not come to be served but to serve, and to give His life as a ransom for many." Luke 22:27 records that Jesus said: "For which is greater, he who reclines at table, or he who serves? Is it not he who reclines? But I am in your midst as he who serves." These words indicate that Jesus as the Servant of Yahweh renders a service at table, but which one? In John 13:12-17 the service which Jesus renders is the washing of the feet; however, Luke makes no reference to this anywhere in his narrative of the Last Supper. The only service which Jesus performs in the Lukan account is the giving of the eucharistic bread and wine. So, from this viewpoint, it would seem that Jesus' action with respect to the food has Messianic significance: It is an act of the Servant of Yahweh, the Messiah. Since this action involves a "giving" by the Servant of Yahweh, the participants of the Last Supper must be receiving a share in the redemptive work of the Servant. The Messianic implications of the essential action of the Last Supper, consequently, are clear from the context of the Lukan narrative.

The Relationship of the Last Supper to the Establishment of the Kingdom

Mark 14:25 (Matt. 26:29) records the vow of abstinence which is to be in force until the eschatological fulfillment: "Amen I say to you, that I will drink no more of the fruit of the vine, until that day when I shall drink it new in the Kingdom of God." This reference to the Messianic Banquet of the Kingdom is placed immediately after the institution of the Eucharist. By means of this juxtaposition the Last Supper is depicted as the last banquet of Jesus with His disciples prior to the eschatological fulfillment; or, to put it another way, the first step in the final phase of the establishment of the Kingdom. For Jesus goes immediately from the supper table to the Mount of Olives and the destiny which He had foretold in the words of interpretation.

Luke, however, has a somewhat different orientation. The vow of abstinence is mentioned *before* the words of institution, and moreover, is expressed in two forms. One mentions the drinking of the fruit of the vine when the Kingdom of God comes (v. 18) and has essentially the same form as Mark and Matthew; the other form of the vow refers to the eating of the Passover when it is fulfilled in the Kingdom (v. 16). From the latter form of the vow, one gathers that the Messianic Banquet, the Banquet of the Kingdom, is the fulfillment of the Passover. The Passover of the Old Law is a type of the Messianic Banquet.

In the Lukan context, what is the relationship of the Eucharist to the Messianic Banquet? We have already seen that the Eucharist is antitype of the Old Pasch according to the Synoptics. Hence, in view of the identification of the Messianic Banquet with the fulfillment of the Old Pasch, the Last Supper would seem to qualify as the Messianic Banquet. The further observation that Luke pictures Jesus as giving the Eucharist as the Servant of Yahweh, the Messiah, strengthens this opinion. If the giving of the eucharistic food and drink is a specific function of the Messiah, it must be the food of the Messianic Banquet. In addition, the fact that Luke places the vow of abstinence before the institution of the Eucharist leads to a similar conclusion.

In Luke the Eucharist is not presented as the last occasion wherein Christ and His disciples share in table fellowship before the eschatological fulfillment. Rather, in contrast to Mark and Matthew, the solemn vow of abstinence is immediately followed by the eucharistic banquet wherein Jesus as master of the household blesses the bread and wine and dispenses this food to His guests. In the Lukan narrative the Eucharist is presented as the fulfillment of the Old Pasch which releases Jesus from the vow of abstinence. The *eating* and *drinking* of the eucharistic bread and wine seem to herald the realization of the *eating* and *drinking* of the Messianic Banquet mentioned in verses 16-18.

This interpretation seems to be required in view of Jesus' statement in Luke 22:29-30. After the words of institution, Jesus tells His disciples that He *gives* or *arranges* for them a Kingdom and that in that Kingdom they may eat and drink at His table. The banquet referred to is the Messianic Banquet, but not a feast, which awaits the definitive eschatological consummation. It is clear from the banquets of Jesus and His followers after the Resurrection (Luke 24:30-31, 41-42) that the Kingdom has come and that the Pasch has been fulfilled in the time of the Church on earth, since the vow of abstinence is not in force. Hence, in view of the fact that Jesus gives the Apostles a Kingdom as a present possession in which the Messianic Banquet is realized, and taking into account the command of Christ to repeat the Eucharist in His remembrance, it seems that a eucharistic meaning must be attributed to "that you may eat and drink at My table in My kingdom" (Luke 22:30).

We have already seen that Luke 22:15-18 is probably an ancient account of the institution of the Eucharist expressed under the form of the cup. Luke has altered this tradition so that it now serves as the introduction to the account of institution which conforms to the other three formulations. On the other hand we cannot completely discount the possibility that Luke may simply have combined the Pauline and Markan accounts to contrast the Jewish

Pasch (lamb and cup) with the Christian Pasch (bread and cup). At any rate, whatever may be the source of the eschatological statements of Luke 22:15-18, it seems that they are employed here to convey the idea that the Eucharist is the Messianic Banquet which fulfills the Pasch and reveals the advent of the Kingdom. Thus, by a judicious arrangement of the text, Luke calls attention to the fact that the eucharistic celebration at the Last Supper was an anticipation of the Messianic Banquet. Even before the completion of the redemptive work (Life-Death-Resurrection-Ascension-Mission of the Spirit) which establishes the Kingdom, Jesus celebrates the banquet of the Kingdom.

This understanding of the Last Supper as a proleptic memorial banquet of the Messianic Kingdom is also indicated in Mark and Matthew, but from another viewpoint. We have seen that Mark and Matthew describe the Eucharist as the last step prior to the eschatological fulfillment, or the first step in the final phase of the establishment of the Kingdom. This concept does not conflict with Luke's presentation of the Eucharist as a meal within the Kingdom. Both accounts simply stress one or another aspect of the Last Supper. Luke emphasizes that the fulfillment to come has been *anticipated* at the Last Supper, whereas Mark and Matthew point out that the fulfillment has not yet come. However, it can be shown that the latter also present the Eucharist at the Last Supper as the anticipated fulfillment of the Messianic Banquet.

The proleptic atmosphere of the Last Supper is prepared for in Mark and Matthew by the narrative which immediately precedes it. Mark 14:3-9 (Matt. 26:6-13; cf. John 12:1-8) describes the anointing of Jesus' head by the woman at the house of Simon the leper in Bethany. This event occurred just prior to His ascent to the Holy City. Jesus interprets this action as an anointing in preparation for burial: ". . . she has anointed My body in preparation for burial." Following this account, Mark and Matthew record seven prophecies made by Jesus. Set in the midst of these prophecies is that which relates to His role as the Servant of Yahweh, who gives His life for the world. This prophecy, spoken over the bread and wine which is then given to the Apostles, takes on the character of a dramatic action and falls into the class of a special type of prophecy frequently encountered in the Old Testament (Ezek. 5:1-5; 4:1-3; Jer. 19:11; cf. Acts 21:11) which is marked by the interlacing of words and gestures. Such prophecies, just as word prophecies, not only establish the truth of a future event but are the very overture of the event. They share in the divine causality; they make visible the divine intention; and since the word of Yahweh "shall not return to me empty" (Isa. 55:11), these prophecies are considered to effect what they express (2 Kings 13:19).

As acted prophecy, the words and gestures of Jesus over the bread and wine are a prophetic presentation of what they signify. Since this ritual gesture expresses the self-giving of the Servant of Yahweh for the redemption of the world, it is the efficacious overture of the final redemptive act. It is the redemptive act in symbolic form. To participate in this ritual gesture by eating and drinking the food over which the words of interpretation have been spoken will, consequently, involve a participation in the fruits of redemption. But to participate in the blessings of the redemption by way of a banquet is to participate in the Messianic Banquet. Thus, seen from the viewpoint of an acted prophecy, the accounts of Mark and Matthew reveal that the eucharistic celebration before the passion was an anticipated Messianic Banquet.

Conclusion

From the context of the Last Supper we have deduced several conclusions which are important for the understanding of the significance of the Eucharist. They may be summarized as follows: (1) *The Eucharist is the fulfillment of the Old Pasch.* As such it has a meaning analogous to what the Paschal feast had in the old dispensation. The Paschal feast included a cultic meal which recalled the crucial redemptive intervention of Yahweh at the time of the Exodus. It was the occasion for the re-presentation, the reactualization, of the saving activity of Yahweh for the benefit of the participants of the feast. The Eucharist as the memorial banquet of the new dispensation involves the re-presentation, the reactualization, of the redemptive work of Jesus for the benefit of the participants of the Lord's Supper. (2) *The institution of the Eucharist is a service of the Servant of Yahweh.* The significance of the Eucharist for the new economy of salvation is heightened by the fact that Jesus gives it formally as the Servant of Yahweh. He institutes the Eucharist in His capacity of redeemer. Hence, the Eucharist is one of the fruits of the redemptive work. (3) *The Eucharist is the Messianic Banquet of the Kingdom.* This characteristic of the Eucharist indicates its intimate relationship with the Messianic blessings. In Jewish tradition the Messianic Banquet is understood as the place where the blessings of the eschatological Kingdom are dispensed. Thus, the Eucharist is the place *par excellence* where the members of the Kingdom receive the Messianic blessings.

The study of the context of the institution of the Eucharist reveals much about the meaning which the Evangelists and the early Church attached to it. But it does not reveal all. To understand the full import of the Lord's Supper, one must turn to the *words of interpretation* which Jesus spoke over the bread and wine. It is through them that we begin to realize the profound nature of this cultic meal.

INTERPRETATION

In our investigation of the four accounts of the institution of the Eucharist we observed that, although they agree on essentials, no one is exactly like the other. Behind the Pauline and Lukan accounts we were able to uncover an ancient formulation which probably served as a common basis for both. Because this Antioch-Palestinian version seems to be the oldest available record of the words of institution, we will use this text as the point of departure for the interpretation of the institutional accounts.

We have indicated two reasons for dating the Antioch-Palestinian account before Mark and Matthew. There is also a third reason based on a theological outlook which is peculiar to this version. In this account the redemptive work of Christ is described as the self-giving of the Servant of Yahweh. In Mark and Matthew it is presented as a cultic sacrifice. Let us consider these different viewpoints in detail, for they not only give evidence of the age of the accounts but have important bearing on the interpretation of the words of institution.

Theological Outlook of the Antioch-Palestinian Account

The reader will recall that the prophet Isaiah describes the Servant of Yahweh as glorious yet called to suffering. His glory comes from the fact that Yahweh's spirit is upon Him (Isa. 42:1), that Yahweh uses Him to preach the message of deliverance (61:1), that Yahweh establishes the covenant through Him with all the people (42:6; 49:8) and gives Him as a "light to the Gentiles" (42:6). At the same time, the Servant is destined to experience failure (49:4) and physical abuse (50:6), but this degradation is only temporary (53). The Servant is a man of sorrows, who has borne our sorrows, who is led like a lamb to the slaughter, who pours out His soul in death and allows Himself to be counted with the transgressors. But since He has undertaken this passion for us in order to make intercession for sinful humanity, He will be rewarded. The time of His exaltation will come and He will see the fruit of His work and be satisfied.

In the New Testament, Jesus is identified with the Servant by the voice from heaven: "This is My beloved Son in whom I am well pleased" (Matt. 3:17). These words recall the statement of Isaiah 42:1: "Behold My servant . . . My chosen, in whom My soul delights." The Evangelists also preserve the words in which Jesus described His coming passion in terms which identify Him with the Servant. In Mark 10:45 (Matt. 20:26), a text to which we have already referred, Jesus says: "For the Son of Man also has not come to be served but to serve, and to give His life as a ransom for many." This passage reflects Isaiah 53, which speaks of the suffering of the Servant in like terms.

With this background, it would be naturally expected that Jesus should present Himself as the Servant in the reference to the passion found in the words of institution. He does this in the Antioch-Palestinian account by referring to His body "which is given for many," thus describing Himself in terms of the Servant given in death and bearing the sins of many (Isa. 53:12). Along the same lines, the words spoken over the cup refer to "the new covenant in My blood." Here Jesus reveals that His suffering ("in My blood") establishes the new covenant associated with the Servant (Isa. 42:6; 49:8). Thus, this form of the institutional account expresses the prophecy of the death of Jesus under the form of the surrender of the person of the Suffering Servant to God in behalf of the people. This manner of describing the redemptive work of Jesus is common in the New Testament. Not only do we find it in Mark 10:45, to which we have referred, but also in The Acts of the Apostles 8:32 and in the Epistles of St. Paul (Gal. 1:4; 2:20).

Theological Outlook of the Mark and Matthew Account

The Mark and Matthew versions have a somewhat different orientation. The words spoken over the bread state simply: "This is My body." One must wait until the blessing of the cup for a further explanation which associates the body with the redemptive work. Moreover, in these accounts the parallel predicates are *body* and *blood* instead of *body* and *covenant,* which we find in the Antioch-Palestinian account. Thus a closer link is established between the two concepts of body and blood. Also the expression "which is shed for you" is added to the words spoken over the wine. Finally the blood is directly related to the covenant rather than through the middle term "cup" as is done in the Antioch-Palestinian version.

The result of these changes is a presentation of the redemptive death of Jesus as a cultic sacrifice. Jesus is depicted in the role of the new Moses who establishes the new covenant by the sacrificial offering of His own blood. The close link between body and blood evokes the idea of the Jewish cultic sacrifice in which flesh appears beside blood but separate from it. In the sacrificial ritual of Israel, the flesh and blood of the victim were separated from one another to provide the material of sacrifice (Lev. 17:5-6; Deut. 12:27). Again the transference of all further explanation of body to the words spoken over the cup emphasizes the blood which is the all-important medium in cultic sacrifice. In this connection, the addition "which is shed for you" alludes to the sacrificial blood poured out around the altar in the Mosaic liturgy (Lev. 1:5, 11; 3:2). Finally, the change by which the blood is directly related to the covenant brings the statement of Jesus into conformity with Exodus 24:8 which speaks of "the blood of the covenant," that is, the blood of the victim of the cultic sacrifice which seals the covenant.

This manner of describing the redemptive death of Jesus is also found elsewhere in the New Testament, especially in the Epistle to the Hebrews (7:27; 9:14, 28; 10;12, 14). St. Paul speaks of Jesus' death as "an offering and a sacrifice to God to ascend in fragrant odor" (Eph. 5:2).

From the foregoing analysis, we have concluded that two theological viewpoints are expressed in the two basic versions of the institutional accounts. In the Antioch-Palestinian account, the death of Jesus is expressed in terms of the self-giving of the Servant. In the Mark and Matthew accounts, the death of Jesus is described more in terms of a cultic offering reminiscent of the sacrificial liturgy of the Old Law. The former is in closer harmony with the way Jesus speaks of it in Mark 10:45. It is closer to the familiar Servant of Yahweh Christology of the primitive Apostolic kerygma (Acts 8:32) and must be judged more ancient than the corresponding Mark and Matthew accounts which show signs of a more developed theological outlook.

The Antioch-Palestinian account notes the orientation employed by Jesus at the Last Supper. The notion of cultic sacrifice stands in the background, but the emphasis is placed on the Servant theme. Thus, the accounts of Mark and Matthew ought to be seen in the light of the Servant of Yahweh Christology. Even though the cultic, sacrificial presentation prevails in Mark and Matthew, it should be understood as secondary and not decisive for the actual interpretation of the words of institution. In this case also, the more ancient way of expressing Jesus' redemptive death should be of primary importance.

The Words of Interpretation (Antioch-Palestinian Account)

In our analysis of the Antioch-Palestinian account we will follow the common method of discussing first the obvious meaning of important words and phrases. Then we will undertake the interpretation of the religious significance of the account.

"In like manner also the cup after the meal": The two consecrations were separated by a meal, from which observation two conclusions can be drawn. (1) The word *body* should have a meaning, appropriate to the context, independently of the term *blood* which was not introduced until the end of the meal. (2) The words spoken over the bread should have contained some expression beyond the cryptic sentence found in Mark and Matthew: "This is My body." The Apostles should not have had to wait until the end of the meal to find out that the body of which Christ speaks is the body *delivered up for them.* Jesus must have used some qualification such as we find in the Antioch-Palestinian account: *"This is My body which is given for many."*

"Body": If the term *body* is to be understood independently of the term blood, it cannot refer to an anatomical ingredient of the whole man. But if it is not to be taken as part of the couplet, body-blood, what does it mean?

The Greek translation of Jesus' original expression is *sōma* (body). We are not sure what word Jesus actually used, nor are we even certain, for that matter, what language He spoke at the Last Supper. Many scholars have taken it for granted that He spoke Aramaic, but He may well have used Hebrew, the *lingua sacra,* on this solemn occasion. The Hebraisms of the Fourth Gospel and the documents of the Qumran community show that Hebrew was not a "dead language" in the first century.

At any rate, prescinding from the dispute about the particular language used, it is not possible to establish with certainty whether Jesus used the equivalent of *body* or *flesh*. Actually the LXX translates the Hebrew word *bāsār* (flesh) by *sarx* (flesh) 143 times, and by *sōma* (body) only 23 times. Some scholars claim that the original word was the Aramaic *gûph* [body (Hebrew: *gûphâh*)]. This was rejected by J. Jeremias on the grounds that Jesus links *sōma* with *haima* (blood) as a twin concept. In this case, according to the Semitic usage, the complement of blood is flesh. Hence, Jeremias maintains that the Aramaic word used by Jesus was *bisrā* (flesh). However, as we have seen, it is not at all clear that Jesus intended to employ the twin concept, flesh-blood.

The use of the twin concept *bāsār-dam* (flesh-blood), translated

in the LXX by *sarx-haima* or *kreas-haima,* was not necessary to
bring out the meaning intended by Jesus, and the evidence at hand
points to the conclusion that Jesus did not intend to use it. This
twin concept, besides indicating the whole man in his transitory
state (Eccles. 14:18; 17:31), is also employed to express the com-
ponents of the body, especially of the sacrificial animal after it has
been killed (Gen. 9:4; Lev. 17:11, 14). Therefore, it is an apt concept to express the redemptive death of Jesus, although the use of
the twin concept usually involves a close juxtaposition of the words
or phrases involved. In the present instance, this use would be more
naturally expected if the blessing of the bread and wine followed
one another without any time lapse. This was not the case at the
Last Supper, however, where the bread was blessed at the beginning
of the meal and the wine afterwards. Moreover, in the Antioch-
Palestinian account, the parallel predicates are not body-blood but
body-covenant. It is also worthy to note that all the accounts of
institution use *sōma,* although *sarx* is the ordinary translation of
bāsār in the LXX. There is, therefore, the strong possibility that
sōma was used because the original Semitic version did not have
flesh but *body.*

Nevertheless, we must reckon with the fact that the Fourth Gospel records Jesus' use of *sarx* (flesh) when referring to His eucharistic body (John 6:54-59). So it is possible that St. John who was
present at the Last Supper bears witness to the actual word used by
Jesus and that the *sōma* usage betrays a Hellenistic influence. On
the other hand, there are a number of reasons which could have
dictated John's use of *sarx.* The development of theological outlook
which results in the explicit portrayal of Jesus' death as a cultic
sacrifice might have induced him to use the sacrificial twin concept.
Again the use of *sarx* may be somehow related to the fact that *sōma*
is used in the Fourth Gospel when referring to a dead body (John
2:21; 19:31, 38, 40; 20:12).

The actual Semitic word used by Jesus, whether it was body or
flesh, does not affect the interpretation of the meaning intended by
Jesus. Whether Jesus used flesh or body, the word signified, not an
anatomical ingredient of His humanity in contrast to soul or blood,
but rather stood as *pars pro toto* for His whole "Ego" in its cor-

poreal epiphany. Taken by itself, unrelated to the concept of blood which would be introduced only "after the meal," the Apostles would have understood, and Jesus would have intended, only one meaning for body-flesh: His whole person. It designates the concrete reality which "is given for many." Flesh and blood or body and blood (though this latter form is not a Semitic twin concept) taken together would have the same meaning, but the two concepts were not linked closely enough at the Last Supper to allow this interpretation.

This use of body or flesh to represent the whole person was familiar to the Jewish mentality of the first century. In the Old Testament, "flesh" designates the visible form of a man, the living form of one's being, the "Ego" in its body-soul unity. Thus, the Psalmist can say: My flesh faints for Thee (Ps. 63:1; cf. Ps. 84:2); and the Greek equivalent *sarx* is used in the Fourth Gospel to describe the historical person of Jesus (John 1:14; 6:52; 1 John 4:2; 2 John 7). The Old Testament uses "body" to designate a corpse, and frequently in post-Biblical Hebrew and Aramaic, under Hellenistic influence, it refers to body (living or dead) in contrast to soul. But it could refer to the whole person in its somatic framework in keeping with Semitic anthropology, which looks on man as flesh. Hence, if Christ used *gûph*, it would have been understood as referring to this concrete, historical person who is "given for many."

This meaning of body-flesh is a common one for the actual Greek word used in the accounts of institution. Both B.C. and A.D. Greek writings attest that *sōma* is used to designate the whole person. Moreover, St. Paul uses *sōma* where it refers to the whole man in his fleshly existence (Rom. 6:12; 12:1; 1 Cor. 6:13). Hence, the Greek translation indicates that the original word used by Jesus stood for the whole person, whether it was body or flesh.

"This": The demonstrative pronoun is used to indicate something which is present. Jesus takes bread in His hands and says: "This is My body." This procedure of Jesus' is analogous to that of the leader of the Paschal meal. The Passover regulations prescribe that the father of the household explain the meaning of the various foods which are employed. In the case of the unleavened bread, for

example, he is bound to say: "Lo, the bread of affliction that our fathers ate in the land of Egypt."

It is not superfluous to stress that "This" refers to the bread, for some exegetes have tried to establish a relationship between "This" and the action of breaking the bread as well as the pouring out of the wine. If that were the case, then "This" would indicate the symbolical breaking of the body of Christ [or the death of Christ, since His bones were not broken (John 19:36)] and the shedding of His blood. However, there is no basis in the text for this interpretation. The context indicates that Jesus is following the custom of the Paschal meal by giving the food a *religious* meaning. Moreover, the action of breaking the bread and pouring the wine does not coincide with the words of interpretation. The words are linked rather with the distribution of the bread and wine. What Jesus gives His disciples is designated as His body and blood.

"Is": The copula "is" does not exist in the Hebrew or Aramaic tongue, but it is understood and expressed in all the Greek versions of the institutional accounts. It seems likely that Jesus would have used the third person singular, which could be used to express the copula when speaking precisely. It has been observed that *hu'* is used in the ancient Aramaic when special emphasis is desired, and so some authors insert it into their reconstruction of the original Aramaic form of the words of institution spoken over the bread: *dēn hu' bisrī*. (In the Mark and Matthew renditions of the words spoken over the wine, a similar Aramaic form would hold: *dēn hu' 'idhmī*.) J. Jeremias rejects this hypothesis on the basis that "there is no reason to distinguish the bread which Jesus handed around from any other bread." This can hardly be considered a serious argument, and the charge that certain scholars have been led by dogmatic considerations to postulate the use of *hu'* might well be leveled at Jeremias; that is, his criticism seems to be motivated by dogmatic assumptions.

"Which is given for many": We have seen that Jesus relates the bread to His body, that is, His whole person. Now He goes on to say that this body is that which is given for many, a reference to His role as Servant who bears the sins of many (Isa. 53:12). Jesus characterizes Himself as a *martyr* in the popular sense of the term: One

who gives His life in behalf of others. As we have seen, this is a familiar way in the New Testament to describe the redemptive work.

"Do this in remembrance of Me": Since this phrase refers to the eucharistic celebration as a whole, it will be treated after the words spoken over the cup.

"This cup is the new covenant in My blood":

"This": As in the case of the words spoken over the bread, the demonstrative pronoun refers to what Christ holds in His hands and gives to the Apostles.

"Cup": In Mark and Matthew, the wine of the cup is designated as the blood of Christ. This blood is then directly related to the covenant: "This is My blood of the covenant." In the Antioch-Palestinian account, the cup stands for the contents, the wine, which is said to be the blood of Christ. Thus, the blood of Christ is related to the covenant through the middle term "cup." We have confirmation that the Antioch-Palestinian version means the same thing as the Mark and Matthew accounts from 1 Corinthians 10:16, where Paul affirms that the cup contains the blood of Christ. The cup was an apt word to symbolize the blood of Jesus which is shed for many. It is an ancient symbol of suffering and is used by Jesus in this sense elsewhere in the New Testament (Mark 10:38; 14:36; John 18:11).

"The new covenant in My blood": Jesus says that the new covenant is established through His blood of the cup. *Blood* evokes the idea of death, of "shedding blood," and so of the passion of Jesus. By using the term "blood," Jesus teaches that His passion is to be instrumental in establishing the covenant. But does the use of the term "blood" indicate that Jesus depicts His passion under the form of a cultic sacrifice? "Blood" naturally evokes the idea of cultic sacrifice—blood was the medium in this form of Jewish worship and was used for no other purpose. Moreover, Jesus relates His blood to the new covenant. In so doing there can be little doubt that He remembered the blood of the victim of the cultic sacrifice on Mount Sinai about which Moses exclaimed: "Behold the blood of the covenant which the Lord has made with you" (Ex. 24:8). At least, the concept of cultic sacrifice is in the

background, and it will be emphasized in the Mark and Matthew accounts where the words of Jesus are brought into strict conformity with the words of Moses. However, as we have already observed, *sōma* is not a correlative of blood. It is not part of the sacrificial twin concept flesh-blood, but stands alone for the Servant of Yahweh. Blood, in this context, should also be understood by itself, and in accord with the Servant motif of the Antioch-Palestinian version, it refers to the person of the Servant who through His atoning death (Isa. 53) brings about the new covenant (Isa. 42:6; 49:8).

The concept of blood standing for the whole person was not unfamiliar to the Jewish mind. The Hebrews saw in blood the substance of life (Lev. 17:11, 14). In Deuteronomy 12:23 we read that "blood is the life." This text does not intend to give an abstract definition but indicates the substance which links individual life to the body. Being the bearer of life, it is personalized in Genesis 4:10; it stands as *pars pro toto* for the whole person. In other texts of the Old Testament this same idea is found, that is, where the whole person is conceived as existing, so to speak, in the flowing of the blood (2 Mach. 8:3; Ezek. 35:6). In the New Testament there are traces of the same outlook. The Council of Jerusalem (A.D. 50) presupposes the understanding of blood as "bearer of life" when it upheld the blood-ban (Acts 15:20); and Judas' confession to the chief priests and elders testifies to the tendency to personalize blood: "I have sinned in betraying innocent blood" (Matt. 27:4).

Hence, the blood of the cup, in the Antioch-Palestinian account, represents the *totus Christus* as Suffering Servant of Yahweh. By way of climactic parallelism, Jesus expresses in more dramatic form the revelation already made in the words spoken over the bread. It is by the shedding of the blood of the Servant that the new covenant between God and man will be sealed.

"The new covenant": In the Greek versions of the New Testament, we find the word *diathēkē* which is commonly translated as *covenant*. In profane Greek literature, *diathēkē* means an arrangement, disposition, which is testamental in character. It can refer to a last will or testament, but in the passage under consideration it

has a deeper meaning. Here *diathēkē* is a translation of *berith,* which in the Old Testament, signifies a psychic communion which may be entered into by equals (individuals or nations) or given or established by a superior with an inferior. It involves a harmony of wills expressed in common views and purpose. David and Jonathan on the individual level (1 Sam. 18:1-3) and Solomon and Hiram on the level of nations (1 Kings 5:12) made a *berith* as equals, sharing in a common will and purpose to which each contributed equally. Zedekiah and Nebuchadnezzar entered into a *berith* reminiscent of the Hittite vassal treaties of the second millenium, that is, involving unequal partners (2 Kings 24:17). In this case, the *berith* consisted in Zedekiah having one will with Nebuchadnezzar, namely that of the latter. The *berith* which Yahweh established with the Hebrews was also of this type: The Hebrews entered as an unequal partner, accepting Yahweh's will and purpose as their own.

In the words of institution, Jesus uses the term *berith* to describe the new relationship which He enters into with the Father. This *berith,* just as that which existed between Yahweh and the Israelites, is initiated by God, not by men. It was the Father who sent His only begotten Son (John 3:16) and who "delivered Him up for us all" (Rom. 8:32). As the Son of God sent by the Father, Jesus initiates the covenant which will be definitive.

But if Jesus is the subject of the covenant as the representative of the Father, He is also subject of the covenant as representative of men (Mark 10:45; Gal. 1:4; 2:20; Eph. 2:13-16; 1 Tim. 2:6; Tit. 2:14; John 10:11). As eternal Son it was impossible for Jesus to enter into any new covenant with the Father, but as the *Incarnate* Son of God He could. As representative of mankind He was able to enter into a new and eternal covenant. The visible sign of this covenant is His "body given for many," His blood shed in death. Through this self-giving the new covenant is sealed, just as the old covenant was ratified with the blood of the sacrificial victim (Gen. 15:9-17; Ex. 24:8ff.).

We may go even further and say that Jesus not only establishes the new covenant through His redemptive work but *is* the new covenant, just as He is the way (John 14:6); the vine (John 15:5);

our justification, holiness, and redemption (1 Cor. 1:30); our access
to the Father (Eph. 2:18). In His own person, as God-man, He
expresses the double movement involved in the establishment of
the covenant. As the Son of God He initiated it. As the one sent
from the Father He invites men to enter into the covenant with the
Father, but He is also the called representative of men. As the head
of the new mankind, mankind of the new covenant, His response
to the invitation which He experiences within Himself completes
the establishment of the new relationship between the Father and
mankind. His response is, in effect, our salvation.

"New": It is not certain that Jesus used the adjective *"new"*
with respect to the covenant, but it is at least implicitly understood. Very likely He had before His eyes the "new covenant" foretold by Jeremiah: a royal and Israelitic covenant which would
involve the forgiveness of the people's sins (Jer. 31:31-34). It is a
new covenant, not in the sense that it has no continuity with the
former one, but in the sense that Jeremiah understood it. For
Jeremiah, following Old Testament usage, "new" means raised to
a better and higher order, so the word "new" qualifies the covenant
which Jesus establishes as the supreme fulfillment of the covenant
of Mt. Sinai.

Sharing the body and blood of Jesus: The Antioch-Palestinian
account does not refer explicitly to the invitation extended to the
Apostles to partake of the bread and wine designated as Jesus'
body and blood. Nor do we find explicit mention of the fact that
the Apostles actually ate the bread and drank the cup. Matthew
and Mark record an explicit invitation with reference to the bread,
and Matthew also mentions a similar invitation concerning the
cup. Mark, on the other hand, notes that "all drank of it." But if
the Antioch-Palestinian account omits mentioning that the Apostles
actually shared the body and blood of Jesus, nevertheless there is an
explicit reference to the actual sharing in the eucharistic tradition
associated with this account. In 1 Corinthians 10:16, participation
in the "cup of blessing" is said to be a "sharing in the blood of
Christ," and the reception of the broken bread is designated as a
"sharing in the body of the Lord."

RELIGIOUS SIGNIFICANCE OF THE EUCHARISTIC WORDS AND GESTURES

(1) *The sharing of Jesus' body and blood signifies the intimate union of the Apostles with the Master in His covenant.*

Sharing the Body: The act of eating bread at the beginning of a meal was considered by the Jews as establishing table-fellowship, and it was a sign of union among the participants. No one arriving after the initial distribution of bread was eligible to participate in the rest of the repast. This symbolism of the bread given by Jesus would have been very familiar to the Apostles, but Jesus adds something new to the traditional gesture. He invites His companions to share the bread which He identifies with His body. This invitation also indicates Jesus' desire for the Apostles to enter into intimate fellowship with Him. The expression would not have been familiar to them, however, although they might well have been acquainted with the description of an intimate union as the sharing of the same flesh. Flesh as the basis of physical brotherhood was an apt symbol used by the Hebrews to express an intimate union of men not based on family ties. In the Old Testament, not only are the members of a family spoken of as sharing the same flesh (Gen. 29:14), but all Israel is said to have the same flesh because of the covenant which establishes a legal-spiritual brotherhood (2 Sam. 5:1; Isa. 58:7). In the same vein, Jesus says that union of will and intention with Him in obedience to the Father makes a man His brother: "For whoever does the will of My Father in heaven, he is My brother and mother and sister" (Matt. 12:50; Luke 8:21).

However, at the Last Supper Jesus does not merely invite the Apostles to become one flesh with Him by entering into an intimate union of will and intention. He gives them the bread designated as His body and tells them to eat it and so enter into this union. The gift of the bread designated as His body is the sign of the union; that is, the sharing of the eucharistic bread signifies union with Jesus. Here a new concept is introduced. The Apostles could understand the symbolism of the sharing of food and drink as a sign of union among the participants of a banquet. They could understand the sharing of the food and drink of a liturgical banquet as a sign of union with Yahweh. But the food was not considered to be a symbol of the participants of the feast or of Yahweh. At the Last Supper, on the contrary, the bread is interpreted as Jesus' person.

Sharing the Blood: Jesus gave the cup designated as His blood of the covenant to the disciples to drink. Again Jesus expresses the desire that the Apostles enter into a most intimate union with Him; and again He expresses Himself in a way which was unfamiliar to them. The Apostles could understand the symbolic use of the term "blood" to express an intimate union. Physical brotherhood was recognized as being based on the sharing not only of the same flesh but also of the same blood (Lev. 21:2; 25:49). Analogously, a group of people with a common spirit could be said to possess a common blood. However, Jesus does not merely invite the Apostles to share the same blood with Him, to form a brotherhood. Rather He gives them the cup designated as His blood, and tells them to drink of it and so enter into this union. The gift of the wine designated as His blood is the sign of the union. The sharing of the consecrated wine signifies union with Jesus.

Here again a new concept is introduced. At any rate the concept would be new for a Jew. The rite of drinking wine to establish a covenant was known in the Hellenistic world since the time of Homer, and among many ancient peoples a solemn covenant was sealed with a rite of drinking blood. This rite established a sacred union in which the participants became "blood brothers." Although the former usage, of drinking wine to seal a covenant, may have been practiced by the Hebrews, the latter one was unknown to them. At the time of the Sinaitic covenant, there was a symbolic sharing of the blood of the victim between Yahweh and the people which appears to harken back to the blood rites of other nations. Moses poured half the blood around the altar and the other half was sprinkled on the people (Ex. 24:6-8). There was no drinking of blood, however, because it was forbidden by Yahweh. Even the symbolic drinking of blood, the drinking of a symbol of blood, would have been sacrilegious to the Jewish mentality.

(2) *The sharing of the body and blood of Jesus signifies the redemptive act.*

The eating of the eucharistic bread and the drinking of the eucharistic wine is, as we have seen, a sign of the union between the Apostles and Jesus. The union of will and intention is made visible by the sacramental rite. Furthermore, the words of Jesus which interpret the meaning of the bread and wine reveal that the participation in this food signifies the bestowal of redemption on the participants. And this whole action (the words and gestures of Jesus), in turn, manifests the offering which Jesus makes of His life for men and the acceptance by the Father which makes the gift possible.

Jesus presents the complete drama of redemption (offering-acceptance-blessings) under the form of the gift of Himself, the Servant of Yahweh, to the Apostles. Although the offering of His life to the Father and the bestowal of salvation on His followers stands in the foreground, the acceptance of the offering is presumed. For to give the eucharistic bread and wine as a sign of sharing in the covenant shows that the self-giving of the Servant is fruitful and therefore accepted by the Father.

(3) *The eucharistic action of Jesus at the Last Supper effects a sacramental actual presence of the redemptive act.*

We have seen that the eucharistic action of Jesus signifies the redemptive act in its totality. Is it then a mere dramatic presentation, a parable in action? The context of the Last Supper will not allow us to be content with this simple solution. The essence of the Last Supper is the fulfillment of the Old Pasch, a Messianic action and an anticipated Messianic Banquet. It is a ritual presentation of the event of redemption, and just as the Old Pasch, it must involve an actual presence of the redemptive act.

This truth is well brought out from a consideration of the eucharistic action of Christ under the aspect of *acted prophecy*. As we have already observed at some length, in the Old Testament tradition the acted prophecy of God's representative is efficacious of what it signifies. Jesus, in the same tradition, prophesies by word and gesture the impending passion and the fruit of the passion, that is, the establishment of the covenant. By this means He manifests the offering of obedience and love which is present in His soul: the essence of the redemptive act. The redemption will be completed in history through the visible suffering and exaltation of Jesus. It is ritually manifested at the Last Supper.

But this acted prophecy, just as its counterpart in the Old Testament, is no mere image of the event which depends on a series of historical causes to bring it to fulfillment. It is rather the overture of an event which depends first and foremost on a special divine intervention. As such it has a share in the divine causality. The event prophesied is already essentially fulfilled; God's intervention is already realized. There only remains the chain of historical causes to make the intervention visible in sacred history. Thus, as acted prophecy, analogous to many Old Testament prophecies concerned with impending events, Jesus' action at the Last Supper effects what it signifies: the offering of the Servant and the acceptance by the Father. It is the efficacious anticipation in ritual form of the redemptive event which will have its historical fulfillment in the actual death and Resurrection of Jesus. Sacramentally Jesus is already the Christ at the Last Supper.

(4) *The eucharistic action of Jesus at the Last Supper effects the sacramental real presence of the redeemer.*

Not only is there a sacramental actual presence of the redemptive act, but also a sacramental real presence of the redeemer at the Last Supper. Jesus intended a relationship between the bread and wine and His person. This relationship is made by the representative of the Father in an acted prophecy which is efficacious of what it signifies. If Jesus relates His person to bread and wine, we should expect this to be a relationship which exists independently of the mind, unless we have clear witness to the contrary.

We must remember that we are dealing with a drama which took place in a Jewish milieu of the first century, in a context in which the words and gestures of an authentic representative of God were considered efficacious. The reality signified would be thought to be present with the sign. This is the way Jesus thought and this is the way the Apostles thought. And since there is no evidence to the contrary, we should accept Jesus' words as signifying a real presence and not a real absence. Jesus offers what appears to be bread and wine to the Apostles as His person. Since there is not the slightest hint of a mere "symbolic" understanding, the sacramental real presence is assured. It is this understanding which was accepted by the primitive Church (cf. Chapters Three and Four).

"Do this in remembrance of Me": J. Jeremias theorizes that these words mean: "Do this that God may remember Me," or "Do this that My remembrance may come before God." This interpretation has been sufficiently refuted by many authors. The invitation of Jesus is grammatically clear and has an unequivocal meaning: He requests the Apostles to do something in remembrance of Him. If Jesus had intended the meaning proposed by Jeremias, He would have spoken in a way which corresponds to the many expressions of the Old Testament in which the remembrance is expressly linked to Yahweh. Actually in the primitive Church, or for that matter in the whole of Christian tradition, one cannot find an example of a prayer in which God is asked to remember the Messiah. The Christian prays to Christ, the Lord. In view of these remarks, we are forced to conclude that Jesus asks the disciples to break the bread and drink the wine in remembrance of Him.

The authenticity of this invitation has been questioned by many scholars. However, some such statement as this must have been made by Jesus at the Last Supper for the attribution to Jesus of the institution of the Eucharist as a memorial of His redemptive death was accepted by the entire primitive Church, including the Apostles who were present at the Last Supper. Some critics have tried to show that this formula was introduced by the Hellenistic Church in an effort to transform the Lord's Supper into a memorial feast of Christ's death. This change is supposed to have been influenced by the Graeco-Roman practice of celebrating memorial banquets in remembrance of the dead. There is a similarity of language between the invitation of Christ and the language of the formulae of the foundation of contemporary Hellenistic memorial feasts, but there the likeness ends. The Eucharist is not a memorial feast of a dead friend but of the living *Kyrios* and His redemptive work.

The memorial aspect of the Lord's Supper resembles rather the religious memorial feast of the Passover. Just as the Passover was a memorial of the redemptive work of Yahweh (Ex. 12:14; 13:3, 9; Deut. 16:3), so the Eucharist is the memorial of the salvific work of Jesus. In the context of the Paschal feast, in all probability Christ made explicit both His desire that it be repeated and its memorial character which makes it antitype, fulfillment of the Jewish Passover.

The omission of the invitation to repeat the rite as a memorial in Mark and Matthew does not seriously challenge the authenticity of the statement. The omission may be due to the liturgical development. Generally speaking, there would be no need to repeat the invitation in the liturgical recital of the words of institution among Christians who understood both that it had been instituted by Christ and that it was a memorial of His redemptive work. Moreover, the very words of the liturgical formulae and the hymnic recitals of the redemptive work (Col. 1:12-20; Phil. 2:5-11; John 1:1-18) which were associated with the eucharistic celebrations brought out the memorial aspect of the Lord's Supper. On the other hand, the explicit command in the Pauline and Lukan versions, which we take to be historical, may have been retained as a means of further instruction for the Hellenistic Church. This possibility is supported by the fact that Paul found it necessary to emphasize for the Church of Corinth that the eucharistic celebration proclaims "the death of the Lord" (1 Cor. 11:26). At any rate, whether the Eucharist was explicitly termed a memorial or not, this characteristic is discernible in all the accounts of institution.

Regarding the statement of Paul just mentioned, the question is frequently asked: Does "proclaiming the death of the Lord until He comes" refer to a recital of the mighty works of Christ associated with the Lord's Supper? To proclaim (*kataggellein*) refers, in common usage, to a proclamation by words. And in the *bārak*, which was an integral part of the eucharistic celebration, there would have been a proclamation by words, generally in hymnic form, of the redemptive work. It seems beyond dispute that the Eucharist was celebrated at Corinth after the agape. It was associated with the final blessing which was spoken over "the cup of blessing" (1 Cor. 10:16). We may then suppose that the eucharistic prayer in which the recital of the institution was inserted took the form of a Jewish table *bārak* and consequently included an *anamnēsis* of the great works of Christ, just as the Jewish *bārak* contained a remembrance of the saving works of Yahweh (cf. Chapter Six).

However, it would seem that *kataggellein* includes also the ritual act itself. Paul links the proclamation to the eating and drinking of the eucharistic bread and wine: "For as often as you eat this bread and drink this cup, you proclaim the death of the Lord until He comes." Apparently, Paul has in mind that the sharing of the body and blood of the redeemer is a symbolic expression of the redemptive work of Christ and hence "proclaims the death of the Lord." The proclamation, from this viewpoint, includes the complex of the *bārak-anamnēsis* and the ritual action.

"Do this": The rite should be repeated in the fellowship of the Apostles, and as Paul says, this ritual proclamation is to continue "until He comes." The phrase "until He comes" highlights the eschatological character of the Eucharist. It is a pledge of the future definitive triumph of those who are in Christ. As such it should be continued until the consummation of the world.

"In remembrance of Me": The concept of ritual memorial was not unfamiliar to the Jews. It played a key role in their liturgy. In their ritual services they recalled the saving work which Yahweh had accomplished in the history of the chosen people. But these memorial rites were not merely a means which served to recall to the Hebrews what Yahweh had done for their fathers in the past. The ritual acts themselves were an occasion for a special objective presence of the redemptive activity which they recalled. The possibility of this objective presence offered no difficulty to the Hebrew mind. For the Hebrew mentality, the acts of salvation history were never really past. Only that which ceased to operate its effect was considered past. In the Hebrew view of time there was a continuity between the present and the past acts of Yahweh in history which enabled the individual and the nation to experience as a now-event the salvific intervention of Yahweh which entered onto the stage of history in the past.

Of the various ritual actions which recalled the saving work of Yahweh, the Paschal feast was the memorial par excellence. It was *the* day of commemoration inaugurated by Yahweh Himself (Ex.

12:14). It was called a memorial [*Lezikkārôn* (Hebrew); *mnēmosu-non* (LXX); *monumentum* (Vulgate)]. The root word *zākar* means "to hold in memory." This does not mean, however, that the Paschal feast merely served to recall to the participants the events of the Exodus. They were certainly reminded of the Exodus, however, as there was a re-enactment of some of the important features of the night of deliverance. In partaking of the Paschal meal, the Jews were reliving in a dramatic way the events of the deliverance. But there was more than a mere subjective recollection of the Exodus event involved in the Paschal feast. As we have already observed, Yahweh's activity in the event of deliverance was reactualized, made present and experienced, by the participants. This redemptive action, continuous with the history of the chosen people, was understood to be vitally relative to the individual and the community, especially on the Paschal night.

To participate in the Paschal feast, to eat the food which the father had related to the meal of the night of deliverance was taken as a means of sharing in the Exodus event. The Paschal feast was understood as involving a re-presentation of the redemptive act of Yahweh. So closely is this remembrance connected with the historical event that the Hebrew could call the memorial feast "the Pasch" (Ex. 12:11). It is the Pasch *in mysterio*. Ordained by Yahweh, it is the revelation of His saving will and saving action. It is a time when Yahweh thinks of His covenant-will in a special way, and such a remembrance involves a special renewal of the ancient salvific act for those gathered around the Paschal table. The recalling of the Exodus event in the Passover feast has the same effect as calling on the divine name (which equals personality, power of God) in sacrifice (Gen. 12:8), which entails a coming, a presence, and a blessing: "In every place where I cause my name to be remembered, I will come to you and bless you" (Ex. 20:24).

Jesus places the Eucharist in the class of memorial feasts. It will, according to His intention, involve a re-presentation of His redemptive work. As fulfillment of the Old Pasch, the Eucharist is the memorial par excellence of the new covenant. It continues to re-present the covenant act of the Last Supper-Cross, just as the Old Pasch re-presented Yahweh's redemptive activity in the deliverance from Egypt. Hence, in a carefully defined sense we can speak of the Eucharist as the memorial gift which Jesus makes of Himself to the Father and the Church. As memorial gift to the Father, it is the objective re-presentation of the self-giving of the Servant. It renders visible on earth the once-for-all sacrifice which Christ offered sacramentally at the Last Supper and which He manifested through His physical death on the cross. But this re-presentation takes place in the Church. The Church is given this memorial gift so that she may actively associate herself with the offering made on her behalf and thus reap its fruits.

It was not only at the Last Supper that Jesus included the visible community in the sacramental actualization of His covenant. The ritual act by which the Apostles were given a participation in the establishment of the covenant remains in the Church. The covenant of the New Law is re-presented each time the Eucharist is celebrated, and thereby Christians are given the opportunity of manifesting their membership in the covenant and deepening their participation in it.

The Pauline Theology of the Eucharist

P AUL RECEIVED KNOWLEDGE of the Eucharist either at Jerusalem (A.D. 36-38) or at Antioch (A.D. 40). In any case we have every reason to think that he would have interpreted it in accordance with the teaching of the Church of Jerusalem. He was in close contact with that community (Acts 9:27; 11:30; 15:4) and compared his doctrine with that of St. Peter (Gal. 1:18; 2:1ff.). His observations on the significance of the Eucharist are, therefore, important not only for an understanding of St. Paul's personal views but for those of the primitive Palestinian Church as a whole. His teaching contained in 1 Corinthians 10:1-22; 11:17-34 also reveals the eucharistic doctrine of the Corinthian Church; for in these passages Paul does not intend to teach a new doctrine, but simply to recall to the Corinthians something they already know. The Apostle to the Gentiles presumes that the Corinthians know and accept the teaching he proposes and which he uses as the basis for solving pastoral problems.

1 CORINTHIANS 10:1-22

In this passage Paul indicates (1) the relationship of the Eucharist to the ethical life of Christians (vv. 1-13) and (2) the nature and effects of the Eucharist (vv. 14-22).

The Eucharist and the Ethical Life (vv. 1-13)

The chapter begins with a reference to the Exodus from Egypt. Yahweh gave two graces to the Israelites: (1) deliverance through water and (2) miraculous food. The Red Sea and the cloud which protected Israel are understood by Paul as a type of baptism: "All were baptized in Moses, in the cloud and in the sea" (v. 2). The food and drink which Yahweh provided are also types. The food was the manna (Ex. 16:13ff.) and the drink was water which came from the rock Moses struck at the command of Yahweh (Ex. 17:5-7). This rock, Paul states, followed the chosen people through the desert. He alludes to a popular legend which pictured the rock as accompanying the wandering people, serving as a source of refreshment. But Paul interprets the rock as a symbol of Christ: "but the rock was Christ" (v. 4). In the Old Testament Yahweh is called "the rock that begot" Israel (Deut. 32:18; cf. v. 4). Paul applies this name to Christ who as God accompanied the Israelites in the desert. He is the hidden rock that provided for the needs of the people, working in salvation history through His divine power even before the Incarnation.

The manna and water which Yahweh and Christ gave to sustain the wandering people are for Paul *"spiritual* food . . . *spiritual* drink"* (v. 3), where *spiritual* characterizes the food not only as miraculous but as a type: The manna and water are really food and drink but have a spiritual meaning. We have already seen in Chapter One that Deuteronomy 8:2-3 describes manna as a type of spiritual food: the word of God. For Paul, manna and water are also types of the food and drink which Christ gives in the fullness of time: the eucharastic bread and wine.

Now Paul observes that although *all* (stressed five times in vv. 1-4) the Israelites were baptized in the cloud and in the sea and all ate of the same spiritual food and drank the same spiritual drink, yet all did not please God. In fact "with most of them God was not well pleased" (v. 5). Because of their sins of idolatry, fornication, and complaints against Yahweh (vv. 7-10), "they were laid low in the desert" (v. 5). This should serve as a lesson to the Corinthians, says Paul: "These things came to pass as examples to us, that we should not lust after evil things even as they lusted" (v. 6).

The argument of the pericope comes to this. If those who received the types of baptism and the Eucharist were not secure from punishment, neither are those who have received the antitypes, the realities. What happened to the Hebrews should serve as a warning:

"Now all these things happened to them as a type, and they were written for our correction, upon whom the final age of the world has come" (v. 11).

This admonition was occasioned by the attitude of some of the Corinthians who believed that they were secure if they had been baptized and had received the Eucharist. The clue to this attitude is found in verse 12: "Therefore let him who thinks he stands take heed lest he fall." It is not enough to have received the sacraments of rebirth and spiritual nourishment. One must live a life conformed to the Gospel. The fate of sinful Israel should serve as a lesson. Just as it was not enough for the Israelites to receive the spiritual food and drink provided by Yahweh and Christ, so it is not enough for the Corinthians to receive the sacraments. They are not magical instruments, but a gift which involves a task: living a life conformed to the law of God.

In this passage the eschatological character of baptism and the Eucharist is revealed. Although they offer a share in the blessings of the Kingdom of God, nevertheless the Christian who has sacramentally died and risen with Christ and received the sacramental nourishment of the body and blood of Christ remains under the sign of the coming fulfillment. The sacrament of baptism is a source of deliverance, and the "spiritual food and drink" of the Eucharist a means of sustenance during the earthly pilgrimage; just as the Red Sea was a source of deliverance for the Israelites, and the manna and water were a means of sustenance during the wandering in the desert. However, the sacraments do not afford men complete victory over sin and definitive union with God. That will come only when a man has lived to the end, conformed to Christ in his heart.

The Nature and Effects of the Eucharist (vv. 14-22)

Paul now takes up the question of eating meat consecrated to idols. In the heathen sacrifices only a part of the victim was consumed. The rest was eaten at a cultic banquet. Moreover, the meat purchased in the market place was, according to the practice at Corinth, often enough obtained from a sacrificial victim. Hence, a case of conscience arose for the Corinthian Christians. Was it proper to eat meat which had been part of a heathen sacrifice? One faction, the "strong," saw no difficulty in eating meat bought in the market place and even partook of the cultic banquets. The other faction, the "weak," questioned whether it was proper to eat any meat. They were not sure that they could partake of meat obtained from the market place since it might be the flesh of a sacrificial victim. And what should they do if invited to the home of an unbeliever, since the meat offered might have been consecrated to an idol?

This case of conscience was discussed by Paul in Chapter 8 of the same epistle. There he laid down the general principle that idols are nothing (vv. 1-6), implying that they cannot affect in any way the meat which is offered to them. From this it follows that the simple fact of eating such meat does not defile the Christian, nor does the simple fact of abstaining from it make one holy. However, the Apostle goes on to say that some of the Corinthians, through ignorance, believe that false gods exist and that the offering of meat to an idol renders it polluted. If these persons, acting on a false conscience, eat this meat, then they sin (v. 7). There is also another way in which a Christian can sin by eating meat sacrificed to idols, continues Paul. The enlightened, those who realize that the idols are nothing and cannot affect the meat, go so far as to take part in sacred banquets in the temples of idols. This practice scandalizes the "weak." It can lead those who are insufficiently instructed to "be encouraged . . . to eat food offered to idols" (v. 10), though their consciences tell them that it is polluted food. Thus, the "strong" become the occasion for the sin of the "weak": "And so by your knowledge this weak man is destroyed, the brother for whom Christ died" (v. 11). The "strong" sin by leading the "weak" back to idolatrous worship and so away from Christ.

In this pericope Paul instructs the "strong" that Christian liberty must respect the brethren and not serve as a stumbling block (v. 9). They must beware lest they sin against the brethren by "wounding their consciences" for this is a "sin against Christ" (v. 12). Let them, therefore, refrain from eating meat if it is a cause of scandal: "Therefore if food scandalizes my brother, I will eat flesh no more forever, lest I scandalize my brother" (v. 13).

Up to this point Paul has not discussed the sin of *communicatio in sacris* which the "strong" commit by participation in the sacrificial banquets of idol worship. Following the common method of argumentation found in his writings, Paul gives the weaker argument for refraining from participation in heathen cultic banquets first and leaves the final crushing one for Chapter 10. In this pericope he states that the "strong" must give up this practice to save their own souls.

This further discussion is concerned primarily with participation in sacrificial banquets. Paul has indicated that it is not allowable insofar as it gives scandal to the "weak," but now he states that under no conditions is it permissible (vv. 14-22). But he will allow, as he implied in Chapter 8, the eating of consecrated meat at ordinary meals as long as it does not give rise to scandal (vv. 23-30).

Paul feels impelled to warn the Corinthians of the danger involved in the participation in sacrificial banquets. He tells them that if they judge reasonably, they will conclude that a sharing in these cultic meals is a sharing in fellowship with idols, or rather with devils. In order to show the logic of this argument, he presents two acknowledged facts for consideration: (1) Through the Eucharist, the Christian attains participation of Christ. (2) In the Jewish cultic meal, eating of the sacrificial meat implies a sharing in the "altar." The conclusion follows that participation in the heathen cultic meals involves a fellowship with devils. Since idols are nothing, this worship is inspired by devils and implies communion with devils. It must therefore be avoided as detrimental to salvation.

THE EUCHARIST IS A CULTIC MEAL   It is clear enough in this passage, as it is in 1 Corinthians 11:17-34, that the Eucharist is understood to be an important ingredient of the agape (fraternal meal). It is an action in which all share. There seems to be a further indication of the social nature of the Eucharist in verse 16. In speaking of the eucharistic cup, in order to distinguish it from the "cup of blessing" of the solemn Jewish feast, Paul calls it "the cup of blessing that we bless." This blessing would be pronounced by the leader at the eucharistic banquet. But Paul uses the plural "we." He seems to be stressing that although the leader says the prayer, he does it as the representative of the community which is gathered. The fact that the words "we break" are used concerning the eucharistic bread, although it was an act performed by the celebrant alone, shows the social character of the action in the same way.

Beyond this, however, the argument of the pericope presupposes that the eucharistic celebration has the character of a cultic meal and that this fact is well appreciated by the Corinthians. For all the argument of Paul, who is going to compare the Eucharist with the heathen cultic banquets, depends on that. The Corinthians know that the Christian cultic meal involves a sharing of Christ; they should realize that the heathen cultic meals involve association with devils and consequently should be avoided: "You cannot drink the cup of the Lord and the cup of devils; you cannot be partakers of the table of the Lord and the table of devils" (v. 21).

SACRAMENTAL REAL PRESENCE OF THE CRUCIFIED AND RISEN LORD
The eucharistic passages in 1 Corinthians are not directly concerned with the discussion of the sacramental real presence of Christ under the appearances of the bread and wine. 1 Corinthians 10:16 is cited so that Paul might contrast the effect of the Christian cultic meal with that of the heathen cultic meal. In 1 Corinthians 11:27 Paul refers explicitly to the presence of the body and blood of Christ in the forms of bread and wine. Yet even here he has another purpose in mind: to appeal to this presence in order to correct the sinful behavior of the Corinthians. Nevertheless, the realism of the Pauline understanding of Christ's eucharistic presence is inescapable.

The reference to the Eucharist in 1 Corinthians 10:16 is in the form of a rhetorical question: "The cup of blessing that we bless, is it not the sharing of the blood of Christ? And the bread that we break, is it not the partaking of the body of the Lord?" This statement indicates that the doctrine is known to all: a formula derived from the words of institution which were in use in the Corinthian Church. It is true that Paul reverses the order of the institutional account found in 1 Corinthians 11:23-25. But this reversal does not mean that the formulation is dependent on an institutional account in which the cup was consecrated before the bread. Paul reverses bread and cup to link the reference to the eucharistic bread more closely to verse 17, where he uses it as a point of departure for a discussion of the relationship of the Eucharist to the Church. The reference to the cup is included, not only for the sake of completeness, but because Paul is going to compare the Eucharist with the heathen cultic meals and finds a parallel in the "cup of devils" (v. 21).

Since we are dealing with a derivative of the liturgical formula of 1 Corinthians 11:23-25, the same sacramental realism found in that formulation should be assigned here (cf. Chapter Two). Paul, therefore, is talking about the sacramental real presence of the glorified Lord under the forms of bread and wine. Some authors, although admitting that Paul speaks of a real presence of Christ in the Eucharist, believe that a distinction should be made between the crucified body of Jesus and the pneumatic body of Christ. Such a distinction cannot be justified. It is not a question of whether there is a presence of the crucified fleshly body of Jesus or the pneumatic body of the glorified Lord. Paul does not know of the presence of the glorified Lord to the exclusion of the presence of the crucified Jesus. The fact that Paul speaks of the presence not only of the *body* but also of the *blood* indicates that he is concerned with the presence of the exalted Lord who is identical with the historical Jesus who redeemed us by His death.

Beyond the arguments drawn from the words of institution, there are other reasons for inferring sacramental realism from this passage. Paul speaks of *"koinōnia* of the blood of Christ" and *"koinōnia* of the body of the Lord."* The expression *koinōnia* with the genitive of *haima* and *sōma* does not mean "fellowship in something" or "fellowship with someone." It means a "participation in something." In this case it refers to a participation in the eucharistic body and blood of the crucified and glorified Christ. Some have argued that *koinōnia* expresses the same idea as *koinōnos* of verse 18. And since the Jews did not share in Yahweh by eating the sacrificial flesh, so also Paul did not think of Christians sharing in the body of Christ. But there is a difference between *koinōnia* and *koinōnos,* and this difference seems to have influenced the use of the two words. *Koinōnos* simply means "partner"; it has a weak meaning. Others have argued that *koinōnia* does not refer to the participation itself but to a "means of participation." However, there is no basis for inserting between bread and body of Christ the concept of "means of participation." What Paul states is that the participants of the Eucharist receive the sacramentally present Christ. The sacramental realism is unmistakable.

Another reason for concluding that Paul and the Corinthian Church maintained a deep-seated sacramental realism may be drawn from the underlying presupposition of verse 17: "Because the bread is one, we the many are one body, for we all share in the one bread." Paul states that through the bread Christians are made participants in the real unity of the one body, the Church ("the many one body" being a Pauline formula for the Church. Cf. Rom. 12:5; 1 Cor. 12:13-14).

Some have maintained that the "one bread" of verse 17 refers to the one loaf used in the eucharistic celebration at Corinth. If this were the case, Paul would be saying that this one loaf symbolizes the unity of the Church. One might possibly argue against this interpretation on the practical grounds that the whole community at Corinth could hardly have participated in one loaf. But a graver reason exists for rejecting this interpretation. Paul is speaking of a real union which is effected by the participation in the one bread. The one bread causes the real unity of the Church; it does not merely represent, as happens at any meal, the unity of the participants who eat it. Now this meaning would be impossible if the bread were only a "symbol." How could a mere "symbol" establish a unity which is completely real? In other words, verse 17 contains a valid statement only if the bread refers to the eucharistic bread of verse 16 and if that eucharistic bread is identified with the body of the crucified and risen Christ.

There is a parallel between 1 Corinthians 10:17 and 1 Corinthians 12:13 which corroborates this interpretation. In the latter verse we read: "For in one Spirit we were all baptized into one body." The "one Spirit" corresponds to the "one bread" of verse 17. The Spirit makes us members of the "one body"; the "one bread" unites Christians in "one body." A like power is predicated on Spirit and bread, which can only be true if the "one bread" is

Christ. The parallel between 1 Corinthians 10:17 and 1 Corinthians 12:13 demands that 1 Corinthians 10:16b be understood to express sacramental realism.

Paul does not refer to the form of the one loaf of bread but to the one eucharistic bread which is Christ. He is saying that there is one undivided Christ in the Eucharist. All, consequently, who partake of the Eucharist, though quantitatively many, are qualitatively, spiritually, one with Christ and His body, the Church. R. Bultmann has justly observed in his commentary on 1 Corinthians 10:17 that the unity of the celebrating community can only be based on the unity of the bread, if the bread is the body of Christ.

We have mentioned that Paul is not directly concerned with sacramental realism in this passage. Neither does he reflect on *how* the presence of Christ takes place. But the sacramental real presence of Christ is clearly presupposed by Paul as a truth with which the Corinthians are well acquainted. This realism had even been interpreted by some in such a way that there was a danger of a magical conception of the Eucharist asserting itself. As we observed when discussing verses 1-13, some people believed that the real presence of the Lord was sufficient to assure them salvation without corresponding good dispositions on their part and a life conformed to the Gospel.

THE EFFECTS OF THE LORD'S SUPPER FOR THE INDIVIDUAL AND THE CHURCH   *Christian is united to Christ:* Paul understands the Eucharist as affording a participation in the crucified and risen Christ; that is, it unites the participant with Christ. The pagan sacrificial banquets, under the influence of the devils, lead to an unholy fellowship with evil spirits. The Jewish cultic meal, as long as the old covenant remained in force, brought about fellowship with Yahweh. So also the Lord's Supper, fulfillment of the cultic meals of the Old Law, brings about union with God, but in a new and more profound way: The union is effected by a participation of the eucharistic Christ who is given to the gathered community.

Unity of the Church effected through the Eucharist: In discussing the sacramental realism expressed in 1 Corinthians 10:16-17, it was pointed out that the "participation in" the eucharistic bread and wine (*koinōnia tou sōmatos kai tou haimatos*) effects not only "fellowship with the Son" [*koinōnia tou huiou* (1 Cor. 1:9)] but the union of the whole Christ: head and body. Through the Eucharist all become one body: "Because the bread is one, we the many are one body, for we all share in the one bread" (v. 17). This verse, a properly Pauline expression, emphasizes the relationship of the Eucharist to the unity of the Church: The Eucharist effects the unity of the Church. Hence, it has an analogous effect to that of baptism (Eph. 4:5; 1 Cor. 12:13). It is true that there remains some dispute about the interpretation of verse 17, but a growing number of scholars recognize that Paul is describing, in an impressive way, the intimate relationship between the Eucharist and the Church.

Among the various explanations of the logical relationship between verse 17 and verse 16b, the following one seems best suited to the context. The latter verse, which speaks of the eucharistic bread as giving a participation in the body of Christ, serves as a background for the parenthetical argument of verse 17 which, incidentally, is somewhat dissociated from the common line of argumentation of the whole pericope. The teaching contained in this verse can be summarized thus:

> verse 17a: The bread is one (the one undivided Christ).
> verse 17c: We share in the one bread.
> verse 17b: Therefore we, though many, are one body (the *totus Christus*).

Many authors have mentioned the possibility that the formula "body of Christ," may have been inspired by the eucharistic terminology of the words of institution. Certainly this designation received its stamp as an authentic Christian expression at the Last Supper. Paul may have used it in referring to the Church because Christians partake of the eucharistic body of Christ and so become the body of Christ.

At any rate, for Paul, the Eucharist and the Church stand in the closest relationship to one another. Not only are both gifts of Christ, not only are both forms of His presence, but both are dependent upon one another by a relationship of reciprocal causality. The Eucharist is dependent for its existence upon the visible act of the minister who blesses bread and wine as the representative of Christ, but who also stands at the altar as the representative of the Church. The Church, on the other hand, is dependent upon the Eucharist as the sacramental source by which the union of all her members with Christ and among themselves is intensified in the process of growing into the perfect realization of the one body of Christ.

1 CORINTHIANS 11:17-34

Earlier in this letter, Paul mentions that divisions had been created in the Corinthian Church which were based on particular attachments to individual Apostles or preachers (1 Cor. 1:10-12). Now he takes up a concrete abuse connected with the Eucharist which resulted from petty cliques (vv. 17-22). The gatherings of the Corinthians for the celebration of the Lord's Supper should have fostered the spirit of brotherly charity but in fact worked against it. The agape which preceded the Eucharist was the occasion for the manifestation of the divisions which existed. It highlighted the disunity of the Church at Corinth and hence fostered the growth of factions. The meal was supposed to begin when all were present, and the food was to be shared in common. Yet the demands of courtesy and charity were ignored. The rich who arrived first began to eat before the poor, who were detained by their daily work (v. 33). Furthermore, they failed to share their abundance with the needy (vv. 21-22). Social differences were not effaced by love but rather emphasized. All this was totally contrary to the spirit of the Lord's Supper: ". . . it is not the Lord's Supper that you eat" (v. 20). The center of attention was not the Lord but the "Ego": "For at the meal, each one takes first his own supper, and one is hungry, and another drinks overmuch" (v. 21). What passed for the Lord's Supper was really a caricature, a grotesque imitation.

The Apostle says, in effect, that he would have preferred to believe that this was not true. However, even considering exaggerations, he judges that the report of these conditions has some basis. He adds that God permits these divisions so that the "approved" may be revealed (v. 19). They are manifested by the fact that they do not include themselves in the divisions, thus giving proof that the grace of God is at work in them.

In censuring this abuse, Paul tells the offenders to leave their regular meal customs at home: "Have you not homes for your eating and drinking?" (v. 22). To bring the practices of a common, profane meal to the Christian agape is to "despise the Church of God and put to shame the needy" (v. 22). These practices reflect a radical failure to recognize the true nature of the Church which is one in Christ and adds to the embarrassment of the poor who are made conscious of their poverty.

Having exposed the misconduct associated with the Lord's Supper, Paul proceeds to recall the profound significance of these gatherings. The Christians do not come together merely to eat an agape but to celebrate the Eucharist, the basic reason for the assemblies. The agape itself is a preparation for the Eucharist. Hence, the conduct at the agape should be in harmony with the meaning of the Eucharist. In verses 23-25 the narrative of the institution of the Eucharist is recalled. Thereby, the Corinthians are reminded that their conduct should be such as to make them worthy of this spiritual gift.

Paul also notes the consequences of an unworthy reception of the Eucharist: "Therefore whoever eats this bread and drinks the cup of the Lord unworthily, will be guilty of the body and blood of the Lord" (v. 27). To be guilty of the body and blood of the Lord will bring down the judgment of God: "For he who eats and drinks unworthily, without distinguishing the body, eats and drinks judgment to himself" (v. 29). This judgment has, as Paul sees it, already manifested itself in the physical sickness and death which have overtaken some of the brethren: "This is why many among you are infirm and weak, and many sleep" (v. 30).

The Corinthians are advised by the Apostle to search their souls (v. 28), to judge themselves lest they be judged by God (v. 31). For they then will be open to the mercy of God who does not reject the contrite of heart and they will be worthy to receive the Eucharist.

In concluding this section of the epistle, Paul returns to the problem of the abuse mentioned in verses 17-22 and gives some practical advice. To remove the sins against brotherly love associated with the agape, the participants should wait until all have arrived so that the meal may be taken in common (v. 33). And if anyone is unduly hungry he should stay at home (v. 34).

Sacramental Real Presence of the Crucified and Risen Lord

A sacramental realism comparable to that of 1 Corinthians 10:16-17 is expressed in 1 Corinthians 11:27-29. However, as noted previously, Paul does not discuss it for its own sake but so that it may affect the conduct of the Corinthians who do not sufficiently reflect on it. Moreover here again, as in 1 Corinthians 10:16-17, Paul does not reflect on *how* the presence of Christ takes place. He does not, as will later writers of the Church, employ the Hellenistic concept of a change of substance. Nevertheless, he does indicate that the forms of bread and wine enclose a real presence of Christ. For Paul, that which was bread and wine is, after the eucharistic blessing, the body and blood of Christ. This has been shown from the analysis of the Antioch-Palestinian account of which 1 Corinthians 11:23-25 is a variant. It can be further demonstrated from a consideration of verse 27: "Therefore whoever eats this bread and drinks the cup of the Lord unworthily will be guilty of the body and blood of the Lord." The "therefore" of verse 27 indicates that this verse is a conclusion to verses 23-26 where Paul gives an account of the institution of the Eucharist and indicates that the ritual act of sharing the body and blood of Christ is a symbolic expression of the redemptive work (cf. Chapter Two). The unworthiness discussed in verse 27 refers to verses 17-22. The misconduct at the Lord's Supper is the reason for the unworthiness of many of the Corinthians. Hence, the abuse at the agape is both a sin against the community and renders the reception of the Eucharist a sacrilege. There is no question in Paul's mind that the body and blood of Christ are actually received by the unworthy. They receive the sacramentally present Christ, but because of their dispositions incur punishment from God. The presence of Christ is independent of the dispositions of the recipient. It is an objective presence.

Although continuing on the same theme in verse 28, Paul adds a pastoral instruction. A self-judgment is necessary to escape the danger of an unworthy reception of the Eucharist. One's dispositions must be in harmony with the deepest meaning of the Eucharist. In the context of this passage, the self-judgment must take into account the social obligations to brethren. Is one's conduct at the agape in harmony with the character of the Eucharist as the body "given for many"? The following verse, verse 29, refers back to verse 27. Both verses are concerned with the dispositions of the recipient of the Eucharist. In verse 27 guilt was attached to the unworthy reception; in verse 29 there is added the notion that guilt leads to a judgment of condemnation.

Again in verse 29 stress is placed on the sacramental real presence of Christ: ". . . for he who eats and drinks unworthily, without distinguishing the body, eats and drinks judgment to himself." In other words, a failure *to distinguish the body* involves the judgment of God. The unworthiness of the Corinthians is due to the fact that they have failed to distinguish the body. Here body refers to the Eucharist. It stands as *pars pro toto* for the whole Eucharist, just as bread in John 6:59 refers to the whole Eucharist, and "the breaking of the bread" in The Acts of the Apostles 2:42 stands for the whole eucharistic action. Paul is talking about the reception of the Eucharist: In the act of "eating and drinking," the unworthy fail to distinguish the eucharistic body. Some have thought that Paul refers to a failure by some of the Corinthians to distinguish the Eucharist from ordinary food and that this is called a crime against the body and blood of Christ. This interpretation is hardly likely since in actual practice the Eucharist, though an ingredient of a festive meal, was clearly discernible. The blessing of the eucharistic bread and wine took place at the end of the meal at a time when, according to the plan of a festive meal, the "cup of blessing" was mixed and the solemn grace-after-meals was pronounced. Therefore, because of the position which the Eucharist had in the festive meal, it would be clearly recognized as a special food. Moreover, it is beyond dispute that the Christians would have been instructed on such a fundamental aspect of the Lord's Supper. Paul, in fact, supposes that the doctrine of the Eucharist is well known to those to whom he is writing. Finally, the context of this passage will not allow this interpretation.

This pericope is not concerned with the sacramental real presence as such but only insofar as it is related to the conduct of the Corinthians. The unworthiness of the participants does not arise from the fact that they failed to recognize the eucharistic bread and wine as something different from common bread and wine; it arises from *their sins against their neighbors.* Having failed to observe fraternal charity which was demanded of Christians, they also failed to recognize that the Christ they received is not merely the Christ-for-me but the Christ-for-many. This failure was due to their own self-seeking which blinded them to the deepest meaning of the Eucharist and which could only lead to condemnation.

To interpret verse 29 correctly, it is necessary to recognize its close link to the previous two verses. We learned from verse 28 that self-judgment was necessary if one is to receive the Eucharist worthily: a judgment which takes into account the social nature of the Eucharist. The unworthiness mentioned in verse 27 certainly is a result of a lack of fraternal charity at the agape. Consequently, Paul teaches that self-searching under God's grace will bring one's dispositions into harmony with the Eucharist as the "body given for many." In verse 28 we are presented with the condition for the worthy reception of the Eucharist which seems to have been lacking to a great extent at Corinth.

In verse 29 it is stated that the reception of the Eucharist "without distinguishing the body" results in condemnation. Such a reception is a sacrilege, as was observed in verse 27: The unworthy reception makes a man "guilty of the body and the blood of the Lord." Therefore, it merits the judgment of God. The close connection between verse 29 and the previous one demands that we interpret "without distinguishing the body" as involving the nonfulfillment of the condition for the worthy reception of the Eucharist mentioned in verse 28. Therefore, "without distinguishing the body" equals *without recognizing the eucharistic body in its specific claim to fraternal charity.* The failure to subject one's soul to self-scrutiny which would bring the inward dispositions into conformity with the social character of the Eucharist, the body given for many, is culpable. In the agape it leads to sins against the brethren which render the subsequent reception of the Eucharist a sin against the body and blood of Christ.

An ominous note is sounded in verse 30 concerning the unworthy reception of the Eucharist. Because of the sacrilegious reception, some of the Corinthians have fallen sick and others have died. Paul is not attributing to the eucharistic elements a sort of magical power which poisons the unworthy. It is evident from verse 32 that he is referring to an action of God: Sickness and death have been sent by God as a judgment. And, incidentally, Paul does not pretend to know the ultimate fate of those who died because of their abuse of the Lord's Supper. He says that they "sleep" (*koimōntai*), a term normally reserved by him for the "sleep of the just."

The Apostle does not, on the other hand, mean to imply that the worthy reception of the Eucharist prevents sickness and death. He is simply observing that the seemingly uncommon experience of sickness and death ought to be attributed to a visible judgment of God on the unworthy reception of the Eucharist. For the unworthy, the Eucharist becomes a medicine of death (*pharmakon thanatou*), in the sense that it becomes the occasion of the judgment of God. For the worthy, however, it may be called medicine of immortality (*pharmakon athanasias*), as indeed it is by St. Ignatius of Antioch, writing about A.D. 110 (Epistle to the Eph. 20). In this latter case it is the cause of the growth in the Trinitarian life.

SUMMARY   The pericope of 1 Corinthians 11:17-34 takes the form of (1) exposition of an abuse, (2) recitation of the liturgical formula of the institution, (3) criticism of the abuse in the light of the liturgical tradition. The criticism takes up the two preceding parts and develops them. A priori, we should expect that "body" (vv. 27, 29) and "blood" (v. 27) would refer to the Eucharist, since there is no textual point of departure for another understanding of these terms except the words of institution.

The teaching of this pericope with reference to the sacramental real presence may be summarized as follows. The self-seeking at the agape meal is a sin against the community (vv. 17-22); it is also a sin against the eucharistic Christ (vv. 27-29), for whoever does not receive the Eucharist in a way consistent with its character as the body-given-for-many is guilty of a sin against the sacramentally present Christ. Hence, Paul demands self-judgment (v. 28) before communion, a judgment which takes into account the individual's conduct at the agape. Is it consistent with the character of the Eucharist as the body-given-for-many? One must, so says verse 29, "distinguish the body," that is, recognize the body in its specific claim to fraternal love.

This passage is a profound revelation of the intimate relationship between love of one's neighbor and love of Christ. One cannot offend against brotherly love without offending against Christ Himself and rendering the reception of the Eucharist, which is the efficacious sign of the presence of the glorified Lord, a mockery and an occasion for the judgment of God. This intimate union between Christ and the members of His body, the Church, treated here and elsewhere in the Pauline Epistles, seems to have been the special preoccupation of Paul from the time when, on the way to persecute the Christians of Damascus, he received in a vision the admonition of the Lord Jesus: "Saul, Saul, why do you persecute Me" (Acts 9:4). To strike the Christian community was the same as striking Jesus Himself. When Paul inquired who it was that spoke to him, the answer came: "I am Jesus, whom you are persecuting" (Acts 9:5).

The Relationship of the Eucharist to the Church

We have just seen that a sin against the poor is a sin against Christ and renders the reception of the Eucharist a sacrilegious act. But this sin against the needy is also a sin against the whole Church, from Paul's point of view.

According to 1 Corinthians 11:22, the result of the asocial conduct of the Corinthians is twofold: (1) contempt for the *ekklēsia tou Theou* and (2) shaming of the poor. Their behavior touches the Church as a whole. The "Church of God" does not refer merely to the community worshipping at Corinth but must be interpreted in the pre-Pauline sense of the community established by God, the new people of God. The contempt for the Church of God may not be consciously intended, but it is a result of the selfish conduct of the rich at the agape.

But how could the conduct of the rich be contempt for the Church of God? One might answer that the failure to observe fraternal charity with a member or group of members of the Church is, in Pauline theology, an offence against the Church as a whole. Although this is traditional Christian teaching, it seems that Paul had something more in mind. He is talking about contempt for the Church which is manifested *by shaming the needy in the liturgical assembly*. In the back of his mind is the concept of the *gathered community* as a self-representation of the Church. Viewed in this light, the cliques and factions which prevent the self-representation of the Church from appearing can justly be accused of despising the Church of God.

But the behavior of the rich is more than an offence against the Church as such and the poor at Corinth, and so an offence against Christ. It is also an offence against the eucharistic celebration itself. In verse 20 it is stated that because of the behavior of certain ones, "it is not the Lord's Supper that you eat." The conduct of the Corinthians hinders the objective placing of the Lord's Supper. If this is true, then the behavior of the rich must exclude a factor which belongs to the essence of the Lord's Supper. That can be the case only if the Church as brotherly community of the faithful is so ordered to the Eucharist that a crime against the Church is also a crime against the Eucharist and vice versa. Thus, the rich show contempt for the Church in that they will not allow the self-representation of the Church to appear at the agape-Eucharist. But this action is also a crime against the Eucharist which creates the unity manifested in the visible gathering.

This interpretation is in keeping with Paul's understanding of the intimate relationship of the Eucharist to the Church found in 1 Corinthians 10:16-17. In that pericope, as we saw, the Eucharist is described as an efficacious means for building up the unity of the Church. The sinful conduct of the Corinthians is, consequently, contrary to an essential aspect of the Eucharist: its role of effecting and increasing not only the union of God with men but the union of men among themselves. It is not only a sin against the Church; it is also a sin against the deepest meaning of the sacrament of the body and blood of the Lord.

Paul's doctrine of the relationship of the Eucharist to the Church is based on the liturgical account of the institution of the Eucharist. There we read: "This cup is the new covenant in My blood" (1 Cor. 11:25). The sacrifice of Christ establishes the new covenant. His death initiates the new covenant which is completed through the Father's acceptance. Hence, Christ's blood can be described as the blood of the covenant. Now this covenant is the basis of the community of those who are in Christ. The Eucharist, which represents and actualizes this new covenant in a visible way for the Church of all ages, effects the union of men with God and among themselves. That the Corinthians would have been acquainted with the idea that the Eucharist, as covenant sacrifice of the New Law, effects the union of the Church seems certain. They knew the relationship of the Eucharist to the unity of the Church. The passing reference to this in 1 Corinthians 10:17 indicates that Paul supposes it is common knowledge. The Corinthians must also have known the only basis for this doctrine, namely, the teaching of Jesus expressed in the cultic formula.

Chapter
Four

The Johannine Theology of the Eucharist

THE FOURTH GOSPEL does not give an account of the actual institution of the Eucharist, although five chapters (Chapters 13-17) are concerned with the events of the Last Supper. There are texts which contain implicit references to the sacrament of the Lord's Supper. The miracle of the changing of water into wine at Cana (2:1-10) is presented as a type of the Eucharist; the parable of the vine and branches is thought by many to have eucharistic overtones (15:1ff.); the miraculous flow of water and blood from the pierced side of Jesus symbolizes baptism and the Eucharist (19:34). However the most important eucharistic text in John is found in the sixth chapter. In this passage the promise of the Eucharist is recorded and it is related to the chief mysteries of the life of Jesus.

PRELIMINARY OBSERVATIONS

Before beginning a detailed discussion of the Johannine theology of the Eucharist as found in John 6, it will be useful to review briefly certain considerations which have some bearing on the interpretation of this chapter: (1) literary unity, (2) source of material, (3) historical context, (4) influences on literary composition, (5) history of interpretation.

Literary Unity

The controversy concerning the composition of the Fourth Gospel has not been resolved in all its ramifications. However, attempts to analyze distinct, divergent sources which have been compiled by a redactor break down under close analysis. Recent research has

shown that there is no theological, linguistic, or stylistic evidence
which militates against the theory of the literary unity of the Gospel. That is, the same theology, language, and style appear throughout. R. Bultmann, among others, claims that a sacramental appro-
priation of the blessings of salvation is contrary to the essential
message of this Gospel, which stresses the primacy of faith. He concludes that all references to the sacraments should be attributed to
the ecclesiastical redactor. Nevertheless, this position is becoming
increasingly unpopular. Today the sacramental aspects of the
Fourth Gospel are accepted with more and more readiness as being
in keeping with the theological outlook of St. John.

It is possible that there were two additions to this book. Although
all manuscripts, early and late, exhibit the same text, John 6 and
21, for example, have certain characteristics which mark them as
addenda to an earlier edition. But whatever may be said for this
hypothesis, there is no solid evidence for postulating a different
author for the second edition; and what holds for the Fourth
Gospel as a whole, holds for the sixth chapter in particular. In
short, there is no convincing argument, either theological, linguistic,
stylistic, or structural, which can demonstrate that this Chapter was
not written by the one author who was responsible for the rest of
the Gospel.

Source of Material

Supposing the literary unity of John 6, the question arises: Is the
discourse on the Bread of Life and subsequent events (vv. 22-72)
based on tradition or is this section a Johannine construction made
in the interest of theological considerations? This question does
not arise in regard to the miracles of the feeding of the five thou-
sand or the walking on water. Both Matthew and Mark attest to
these miracles; but only John recalls in detail a rather long discourse which was associated with the feeding miracle and the option
of the disciples which was linked to this discourse.

We can find a possible answer to this question in the parallel
passage of Mark 6:30–8:31 which gives some indication of the events
subsequent to the feeding miracle which are recorded in John 6.
The basic scheme of Mark 6:30–8:31 is as follows:

1. first multiplication of loaves and fishes (6:34-44),
2. walking on water (6:45-51),
3. failure of the disciples to understand the meaning of the miracle (6:52),
4. series of dialogues and miracles (6:53–7:37),
5. second multiplication of loaves and fishes (8:1-9),
6. boat journey and discourse with Pharisees about a sign from heaven (8:10-12),
7. boat journey and discourse with disciples about the meaning of feeding miracles (8:13-21).

The first thing to notice is that the second feeding miracle is followed by a boat journey and a discussion with the Pharisees concerning a sign from heaven. This sequence is verified in John 6:30-31. In both cases the reference to the sign from heaven refers to the manna which, according to Jewish tradition, will be given by the Messiah when He makes His appearance at the time of Passover. The second point to observe is that after the discourse with the Pharisees, Jesus gets into a boat with the disciples and, during the crossing of the sea, engages them in a discussion about the leaven of the Pharisees (that is, their teaching), the meaning of the feeding miracles as signs, and the inability of the disciples to interpret these miracles. The warning against the leaven of the Pharisees seems to refer to their opposition to Jesus' teaching. Such opposition is verified in John 6:27-52. The reference to the meaning of the feeding miracles as signs relating to Jesus' person is also brought out in John 6:27-59. The inability of the disciples to understand the meaning of the feeding miracles parallels the lack of faith of some of Jesus' disciples mentioned in John 6:60-67. Finally, the unique saying about the "one loaf" in Mark 8:14 is probably a reference to Jesus Himself and suggests that the discussion with the Pharisees was about the bread of life which Jesus identifies with Himself, as He does in John 6:27-59.

Thus, the discussion with the Pharisees about the sign from heaven, the reference to the "one loaf," the warning against the teaching of the Pharisees, the discourse on the meaning of the feeding miracles, and the inability of the disciples to understand indicate that the tradition on which Mark depends contained traces of a discourse which is recorded at length in John 6:27-59 and of the crisis of faith which is mentioned in John 6:60-72.

It is even possible that the two feeding miracles related in Mark are two accounts of one miracle. Mark 6:52 refers to the lack of understanding of the disciples concerning the first feeding miracle. The phrase "because their hearts were blinded" is repeated in the dialogue following the second feeding miracle (8:17), but occurs nowhere else in this Gospel. This observation indicates that Mark 6:34-52 probably belonged originally with the demand for a sign, the conversation in the boat, the question of faith in Jesus, and the function of the feeding miracle as a sign (8:10-21). If we couple this with the fact that the material which follows Mark 6:34-52 contains a series of incidents which do not belong together, as is indicated by the confusing geographical details, the possibility grows that the first feeding miracle was originally linked with Mark 8:10ff., and that the second feeding miracle is only a different account of the same miracle which was included in the basic traditional material on which Mark built his narrative.

This discussion brings us to the scheme of John 6. One can argue that John follows the original arrangement of the traditional material and gives special emphasis to the discourse on the bread of life in accordance with his over-all plan. But whatever may be said of John's fidelity to the original material, the basic scheme of John 6 is reflected in Mark. Hence, we are not dealing with a Johannine construction which arose simply from theological considerations.

There is one point which Mark does not bring out in his narrative and which is crucial for John 6. According to Mark, the discourse linked with the feeding miracle concerned Jesus' interpretation of it as a sign of the meaning of His person. This interpretation was opposed by the Pharisees and caused Jesus to warn the disciples against their teaching. It was also met with unbelief by the disciples. Hence, we have an indication that the original bread-of-life discourse dealt with the subject of faith in the person of Jesus. But there is no indication in Mark that the original discourse was explicitly concerned with the Eucharist. In John 6:54-59 the Eucharist is mentioned explicitly. Mark's silence on the question of the Eucharist may be significant for the interpretation which we will propose in answer to the question: *Was the Eucharist the subject of the option in the historical bread-of-life discourse?*

Historical Context

A number of details in John 6 are in accordance with the historical setting in which they are given. The Passover date (v. 4) agrees with the observation that there was "much grass" in the place. Being Spring, there would still be grass in the area. The Markan narrative of the first feeding miracle agrees with this date, as is indicated by the reference to the fact that there was "green grass" for the people to sit on (Mark 6:39). The reference to the "leaven of the Pharisees" in the account of the second feeding miracle (8:15), a unique expression in Mark, is also in keeping with the Passover imagery. At that time the old leaven was thrown out as being impure to make way for the new leaven.

There are other details, too, which harmonize with the Passover date in John. The crowd reacted to the feeding miracle by attempting to make Jesus king. It is likely that they saw in this miracle the fulfillment of the traditional belief that the Messiah would manifest Himself at the Passover by giving manna to the people. Finally, the discourse on the bread of life which took place in the synagogue is in keeping with the Passover context. During the Passover the narrative of Yahweh's saving acts at the time of the Exodus was the central topic of the liturgical readings. This means that the subject of manna came into prominence, and in fact, Joshua 5 was read during the Passover week. This chapter relates how the Israelites ate manna for the last time before entering the promised land. According to the rabbinical tradition, this manna remains in a heavenly place until the Messiah's coming in the month of Nisan (cf. Chapter One). Hence this text, or a similar one, would have provided a natural starting point for the bread-of-life discourse, which contrasts the manna of the desert and the bread which Jesus gives.

In view of the foregoing evidence, there is every reason to believe that Jesus was active in Galilee during one Passover season (the year before His death according to Johannine chronology) and performed a miracle for a crowd which may have been on its way to Jerusalem to celebrate the feast. Afterwards He was involved in a discussion with some who had witnessed the miracle in the synagogue of Capharnaum on the Saturday preceding the Passover. The topic of the dialogue was the meaning of the feeding miracle in relation to the manna of the desert. In the course of the discussion He revealed Himself as the bread of life. Moreover, the miracle of the walking on the water probably occurred at this time, as tradition firmly asserts.

Influences on Literary Composition

Various influences played a part in the literary composition of John 6: (1) Old Testament, (2) liturgy, (3) polemical interest.

OLD TESTAMENT   The Fourth Gospel does not usually cite texts from the Old Testament. The author uses the Scriptures in a more comprehensive way. Quotations such as those in John 1:29 involve several passages and metaphors taken from the Old Testament which summarize much of the witness of revelation to the significance of Jesus. The themes of the shepherd and the vine, used in the Old Testament several times and in different ways are reworked by John so that the separate features form a single picture to reveal an important aspect of the meaning of Jesus' person (John 10:1-6; 15:1ff.).

Examples of John's comprehensive use of the Old Testament in John 6 are not difficult to find. The themes of manna, Messianic Banquet, and the banquet of Wisdom are inserted with great skill into the narrative. Many scriptural texts appear to have influenced the composition of sections of this chapter. For example, there is some likelihood that 2 Kings 4:42-44 has influenced the structure of John 6:9-13. Above all, the Exodus motif permeates the Chapter and exerts the most important influence on the literary form of the narrative.

At the outset, Jesus is depicted as the new Moses who "went up the mountain, and was sitting there with his disciples" (v. 3). This action can be compared to that of Moses ascending Mt. Sinai (Ex. 19:3) with the elders to participate in a sacred banquet (Ex. 24:9-11). The crowd wandering in this desert place without food recalls the Israelites who were also without food in the desert. Jesus feeds the crowd as did Moses. The *murmuring* crowd mentioned in verses 41-42, 62 recalls the Israelites who murmured in the desert (Ex. 15-16). There are numerous references to the manna and to the fathers of the desert.

There is similarity between the words used in John's account of the feeding miracle and the LXX version of the Exodus account of the feeding of the Hebrews in the desert. In John 6:12, *eneplēsthē-san* is used to indicate that the crowd had as much as they wanted to eat. This word is used in the same context in Exodus 16:12 (cf. Ps. 78:29), whereas the Synoptics use *exortasthēsan*. Again in John 6:12, Christ tells the disciples to "Gather *(synagagete)* the fragments." The same word is used by Yahweh when commanding the Israelites to take up the manna: "Gather *(synagagete)* of it, every man of you, as much as he can eat" (Ex. 16:16). The Synoptics, on the other hand, use *ēran*.

There are striking parallels between Deuteronomy 8:2-3 and John 6:4-14, which may be summarized as follows:

DEUTERONOMY 8:2-3	JOHN 6:4-14
Crowd wandering in the desert.	Crowd wandering in a desert place (east of the Sea of Genesareth).
Yahweh tests *(ekpeirasē)* Israel before feeding them.	Jesus tests *(peirazōn)* Philip before giving food to the crowd.
Supreme goal of the manna is to teach Israel that the word of Yahweh is the indispensable nourishment.	Supreme goal of the feeding miracle is to teach the crowd that the word of God is the indispensable nourishment in both His teaching and sacramental presence (vv. 26-59). This doctrine is alluded to in the feeding miracle by the stress which is placed on the miracle of the remains: a type of imperishable bread. (This point will be discussed in detail when we consider verses 12-13.)

One final point to note is the influence of the Exodus account of Psalm 78 on John 6. We know that this psalm was uppermost in

John's mind since verse 31 refers to Psalm 78:24 in a quotation which appears to draw also on Nehemiah 9:15. This merger agrees with John's practice of fusing several Old Testament passages together. Comparing the pertinent passages of Psalm 78 and John 6, we obtain the following results:

PSALM 78	JOHN 6
The Israelites tempt Yahweh (18, 41, 56),	Galileans test Jesus (30-31),
"by demanding the food they craved" (18).	by demanding a type of manna: "Bread from heaven He gave them to eat" (31; cf. Ps. 78:24).
Can He also give us bread or provide meat for His people?" (20)— this is a question asked by unbelievers (22).	The request is made by those who have no faith (36).
The Israelites were unmoved by the *sēmeia,* the wonderous works of Yahweh (41-43).	The Galileans were unmoved by the *sēmeia,* the wonderous works of Jesus (26).
The Israelites turned away from Yahweh (57).	The disciples turned away from Jesus (67).
Yahweh rejects the unbelievers (67).	Jesus rejects the unbelievers and Judas (65-67, 72).
Yahweh chooses (*exelexato*) the tribes of Judah and David (67-70).	Jesus chooses (*exalexemēn*) whom He wishes (71).

As was previously indicated, we cannot expect to find a single Old Testament passage which serves as the model for the literary presentation of John 6. The Old Testament is used in a much freer way. Yet it would seem that Psalm 78 played a special role in the composition of this chapter. It is quite likely that Psalm 78 influenced the composition of the bread-of-life discourse to the extent that verses 32-59 are a midrashic commentary on the reference to the manna miracle in the quotation from Psalm 78:24: "Our fathers ate manna in the desert; as it is written, 'He gave them bread from heaven to eat'" (v. 31). Following the midrashic method, the discourse of Jesus after verse 31 pays special attention to each of the words of the scriptural text. In verses 32-59 the words "bread," "from heaven," "he gave," and "eat" are amplified. There are also other clues that John is following the techniques applied in midrash. There is the midrashic method of spiritualization, that is, the explanation of a concrete image in the original text in a spiritual sense. Furthermore, following a very familiar midrashic method, a second meaning is given to the word "bread." The concrete concept of bread is interpreted first in a spiritual sense as the word of revelation. Afterwards a new spiritual meaning is given. Bread now becomes the image of the Incarnate Son of God in His eucharistic presence.

John 6:32-59 falls into the class of a "covert midrash"; that is, although not explicitly stated, verses 32-59 interpret Psalm 78:24 according to the techniques applied in midrash. This is an important point, for it shows the literary unity of the bread-of-life discourse. We have already observed that R. Bultmann claims that references to the sacraments in the Fourth Gospel are interpolations. Hence, he rejects John 6:52-59 as the product of a late redaction. But if verses 32-59 are a midrashic commentary on the text of Psalm 78:24, then verses 52-59 must be included in the original text. Only in these latter verses does the word "eat" receive a development comparable to the treatment given the other words in Psalm 78:24.

LITURGY   The question of the influence of Jewish and Christian liturgical sources on John 6 has been discussed frequently in recent years. In this connection there is more or less general agreement that a concise formulation of the words of institution, similar to that found in Matthew 26:26-28 (Mark 14:22-24) played an important role in the formulation of certain passages of John 6. Just as do the Synoptic accounts of the feeding miracle, John 6:11 portrays Jesus' action in a way which is reminiscent of the Last Supper: "Jesus then took the loaves and when He had given thanks (*eucharistēsas*), distributed them to those reclining." The same eucharistic terminology is found in verse 23, where again the act of giving thanks (*eucharistēsantos*) is linked *only* to the bread and where no mention is made of the distribution of the fish. The Synoptic narratives of Jesus' action in the feeding miracles adhere more closely to the actual words of the accounts of institution, stating that Jesus "broke" (*kateklasen*) the loaves. John omits mention of this action. Nevertheless, by portraying Jesus Himself as feeding the crowd, John's account parallels more closely the activity of Jesus at the Last Supper. In the Synoptic accounts Jesus gives the bread to the disciples and they give it to the crowd. In John it is simply recorded that Jesus distributed the loaves to those reclining. There is, of course, no contradiction between the Synoptics and John in this matter. The large crowd was actually fed by the disciples. John merely stresses that they are but instruments of the Master who really feeds the crowd by the miraculous multiplication of the loaves, which is a type of the Eucharist.

Verse 52b alludes to the words which Christ spoke over the bread in the Pauline and Lukan accounts of the institution: ". . . and the bread I will give is My flesh for the life of the world." Above all the sacramental language of verses 53-59 is inescapable. The words "to eat My flesh and drink My blood" are an explicit reference to the double consecration which took place at the Last Supper. (The problem of the relationship between these verses and the words of institution will be taken up in detail in the section of this chapter called "A Historical Problem.")

When we turn to the subject of the relationship between the Jewish Passover liturgy and John 6, the investigation becomes quite complex. It is likely that the Passover liturgy, which was dominated by the theme of the Exodus, influenced the use of this motif throughout John 6. This influence, however, was probably not direct. There is good reason to believe in the existence of a primitive Christian Passover ritual modeled on the Jewish counterpart which goes back to the time of the composition of the Fourth Gospel. Hence, we are led to the probable conjecture that John 6 was influenced by the intermediary Christian ritual. It is even possible that John 6 served as part of a Christian Passover Haggadah which was closely related to its Jewish antecedent. However, since this hypothesis is not crucial to the interpretation of this chapter, we will omit a detailed investigation of it. What is important to keep in mind at this juncture is that John sets the chapter within the context of the history of salvation wherein Jesus is depicted as fulfilling Old Testament types (Moses, manna) in the *atmosphere of the Last Supper*.

POLEMICAL INTEREST   The unusual language of John 6:54-59 has been discussed by all writers who have treated this pericope. The stark realism of this extremely powerful passage is astonishing. Not only does Jesus speak of the eating of His flesh and the drinking of His blood, but He repeats the statement three times, and adds for good measure, "My flesh is food indeed and My blood is drink indeed." Such a presentation leads one very naturally to conclude that John has reworked the original tradition with a polemical intention. But is there any reason for postulating a polemical influence on this passage?

The existence of Gnostic heretics in the Church is mentioned in the Pauline Epistles. They commonly professed that matter is by its nature evil and the cause of sin. According to this principle, it would be impossible to admit the concept of a sacrament, the Incarnation of the Son of God or the resurrection of the flesh. That they carried out this principle to its logical conclusion is shown by the references which Paul makes to the false teachers who deny the resurrection of the body (1 Cor. 15). Moreover, not long after the composition of the Fourth Gospel, Ignatius testifies that certain Gnostics abstain from the Eucharist because they do not believe that it is the body and blood of Christ (Epistle to the Smyrnaeans 6). From this evidence we have grounds for postulating that a polemical interest influences John 6:54-59: a protest against those who were in principle and in fact denying the value of the Eucharist.

The possibility of a polemical interest in this pericope is heightened by the testimony of Irenaeus, who refers to the traditional belief that the disciples of St. John begged him to write a Gospel against Gnostic teachers who were spreading falsehood concerning the creation of the world and the Incarnation of the Word (*Adversus Haereses* 3:11,1). Finally, if John 6:54-59 is studied in connection with 1 John 5:6-8, a passage of an epistle written against the Gnostic heresies of the day, a polemical intention seems quite plausible.

The text of 1 John 5:6-8 reads: "This is He who came by water and blood, Jesus Christ, not with the water only but with the water and the blood. And the Spirit is the witness, because the Spirit is the truth. There are three witnesses, the Spirit, the water, and the blood; and these three agree." In verse 6 water and blood refer to the baptism and crucifixion of Christ, as the past tense "He who came (*elthōn*)" shows. But verse 8 speaks of the water and the blood as bearing witness at the present time (*martyrountes*) and so must refer to baptism and the Eucharist. Thus, the sacraments are described as re-presenting the redemptive action present in Christ's own baptism and crucifixion. This theory is in harmony with the Johannine concept of the sacraments as continuations of the redemptive work of Christ in the life of the Church. This stress on the blood of Christ in a letter written against false teachers appears to be directed against a Gnostic group in whose dogmatic system the sanctifying blood of Christ (1 John 1:7) had no place. It is likewise reasonable to suppose that the challenge of John 6:54-59 was aimed at the same Gnostic tendency.

We have suggested that the literary form of John 6:54-59 was inspired, at least in part, by the Gnostic rejection of the Eucharist at the end of the first century. But can we say more? Is it possible that the explicit mention of the Eucharist in the bread-of-life discourse was due to the catechetical and polemical interests of the author of the Fourth Gospel? If this were the case, John would be making explicit what Christ implied in the historical discourse and which He revealed at the Last Supper. The answer to this question will be discussed in the section of this chapter called "A Historical Problem."

History of the Interpretation of John 6:54-59

Early in the patristic period, Clement of Alexandria and Origen treated John 6:54-59 as though it referred only to the nourishment of man's soul with the word of Christ's teaching. They do not envision a eucharistic reference. This interpretation, however, is not the common one presented by the Fathers of the Church. Throughout the patristic period there is almost unanimous consent that John 6:54-59 refers to the sacrament of the Lord's Supper.

This interpretation was not seriously challenged by exegetes or theologians within the Catholic Church until the period just before the Council of Trent. The departure from the traditional eucharistic interpretation was occasioned in great part by the appeal of the followers of John Huss to this text to refute what they thought was a distortion in eucharistic practice. In the period contemporaneous with St. Thomas, the custom of administering the Eucharist to the laity under one species came into vogue in the West. There was ample precedent for this practice. For many hundreds of years infants had been given the Eucharist in the form of the consecrated wine alone; and in the early Church, eucharistic bread was commonly kept in the home for daily communion. However the Hussites would not admit this practice and appealed to the words of Christ as recorded in John 6:54-59, which they interpreted as requiring the reception of both species.

Against this contention, Pope Martin V issued the Bull *Inter cunctos* on February 22, 1418, which defended the practice of giving communion under one species to the laity. However, the problem of reconciling John 6:54-59 with this practice continued.

Just before the Council of Trent, Cajetan, a Catholic theologian of great repute, answered the objection of the Hussites by simply denying that the verses in question concerned the Eucharist. According to him, verses 54-59 refer uniquely to union with Christ through faith and love. This interpretation was not acceptable to most Catholic scholars, and so the problem was brought up at the Council of Trent when it discussed the practice of the reception of the Eucharist under one species.

In its definitive teaching, the Council judged that the passage of John 6:54-59 cannot be interpreted as a command to receive under both species, adding this qualification: "However, it may be understood according to the various interpretations of the holy Fathers and doctors." This clause, found in the first chapter of the decree of Session XXI, is important for it shows that the Council did not desire to settle the question of whether or not John 6:54-59 actually refers to the Eucharist.

The reason for this reluctance to settle the question is found in the records of the Council leading up to its final statement which was made on July 16, 1562. In an earlier form of the decree, presented on July 4, 1562, is this statement: "For although following many Greek and Latin Fathers it must be conceded that the words of this chapter pertain to the sacrament of the Eucharist: however it cannot be deduced from the words spoken that the Lord commanded that the bread must be eaten and the cup drunk." This assertion was opposed by a small but articulate group on July 8 for the following reason: *"Ne doctores damnentur."* Hence on July 14, a new text appeared and the phrase concerning the affirmation of the eucharistic teaching of John 6:54-59 was omitted. The clause "Howsoever, it be understood . . ." was added to satisfy all. Thus, a condemnation of Cajetan's position was avoided.

After the Council of Trent, the more traditional view prevailed. Maldonatus, the seventeenth-century theologian and exegete, wrote a good defence of the eucharistic interpretation of John 6. Not content with the interpretation of the text, he cited many Church Fathers to show the moral unanimity of patristic literature on this point. Today Catholic scholars unanimously agree on a eucharistic interpretation of John 6:54-59. Pope Leo XIII in his encyclical *Mirae Caritatis* did not hesitate to use the text to explain eucharistic doctrine.

A somewhat similar evolution has taken place in Protestant writings since the time of the Reformation. The Reformers (Luther, Calvin, and Zwingli) interpreted John 6:54-59 in a figurative sense. They saw in these words a reference to Christ's passion and the necessity for receiving Him by faith. This opinion was accepted by most Protestant theologians and exegetes for over three hundred years. Today, however, the majority of Protestant scholars working in the field admit the sacramental interpretation. In general, only the most conservative theologians and exegetes of the Confessional Churches still cling to the classical Reformation viewpoint.

INTERPRETATION OF JOHN 6

The heart of this chapter is contained in verses 54-59: the promise of the Eucharist. What goes before and what comes after must be seen in the light of these verses. In other words, from the beginning to the end, the thought of this passage is focused on the

Eucharist. Perhaps this chapter could be characterized as a eucharistic catechesis. It resembles the mystagogical catecheses of the fourth-century Church Fathers which served to acquaint the newly baptized Christians with the full significance of the sacraments or "mysteries" which they had already received. The author of the Fourth Gospel supposes that Christians know of the institution of the Eucharist and are receiving the body and blood of the Lord in the weekly celebration of the Lord's Supper. He is not, therefore, concerned with relating the fact of the institution of the Eucharist. Instead, he takes the opportunity to give a rather complete instruction on the meaning of the Eucharist in relation to the central mysteries of the Christian economy of salvation.

Basing the exposition on the events and sayings associated with Jesus, John develops his theme in a way analogous to that of the processing of a photographic plate in which the image, present from the beginning, becomes gradually clearer. That which is seen in a confused way at the outset is revealed in all its details at the end. Consequently, no part of this chapter should be omitted from our study. Each section, almost every sentence, contributes to the Johannine understanding of the Eucharist within the framework of the total Christian revelation.

The chapter is divided into four major sections: (1) the miracle of the multiplication of the loaves and fishes and related events, (2) the miracle of the walking on water and related events, (3) the discourse on the bread of life, and (4) the reaction of the disciples and related events. Before beginning our study of the text, it will be useful to present a more detailed outline which will serve as the framework of our analysis.

OUTLINE OF JOHN 6. 1-72

    I. Miracle of the multiplication of the loaves and fishes and related events (1-15).
       A. Miraculous feeding (1-11).
       B. Miraculous superabundance (12-13).
       C. Reaction of the crowd and the withdrawal of Jesus (14-15).
    II. Miracle of the walking on water and related events (16-25).
       A. Miracle of the walking on water (16-20).
       B. Miraculous arrival at the shore (21).

I. *Miracle of the Multiplication of the Loaves and Fishes and Related Events* (1-15)

A. MIRACULOUS FEEDING (1-11)   We have already seen that John
6 is influenced in its literary form by the Old Testament texts related to the Exodus event, especially in the case of the feeding
miracle. John relates this miracle to that of the miraculous feeding
of the Israelites with manna in the desert. Now since manna was
considered a type of the Eucharist in the primitive Church, as 1
Corinthians 10:3ff. attests, it would seem likely that John views the

feeding miracle as a eucharistic type. This conclusion is confirmed by an analysis of the text.

When discussing the liturgical influences on John 6, we mentioned some evidence which points to the influence of the words of institution on the feeding miracle. Now we shall discuss this relationship in more detail. First, the narrative begins with a reference to the proximity of the Passover (v. 4). This is not mentioned in the Synoptic accounts and at first glance seems to be included as a mere historical note. However, in view of John's style, we would be well advised to look for a symbolic meaning, just as we do in the reference to the fact that "it was night" when Judas left the supper chamber to betray Jesus (13:30). It is likely that John wished to establish a eucharistic atmosphere from the beginning. The approaching Paschal feast is the last, according to Johannine chronology, before the death of Jesus. On the next one He will give, not the miraculous bread, but His eucharistic flesh and blood.

The eucharistic significance is heightened by the fact that the multiplication of the loaves and fishes occupies the whole scene. This miracle is not pictured as the climax of a day of curing the sick and teaching as it is in the Synoptic accounts (Matt. 14:14; 15:29-31; Mark 6:34; Luke 9:11). The impression is given that Jesus is there simply to nourish the crowd with miraculous food. Accordingly, Jesus takes the initiative: "When, therefore, Jesus had lifted up His eyes and seen that a very great crowd had come to Him, He said to Philip, 'Whence shall we buy bread that these may eat?' " (v. 5). In the Synoptic accounts it is the disciples who initiate the movement which results in the feeding miracle (Matt. 14:15; Mark 6:35; Luke 9:12). They implore Jesus to send the crowds away so that they might obtain food from the villages nearby.

Again in John's account, Philip does not ask whether the disciples should purchase 200 denarii worth of bread as Mark 6:37 relates. He simply says that this sum would not suffice to buy enough food so that all could eat (v. 7). John would seem to be emphasizing here that human power alone cannot satisfy the hunger of these people. In this same connection, Andrew asks what five barley loaves will avail among so many (v. 9). The mention of barley loaves, by

John alone, would seem to be more than a mere historical note. It appears to be a conscious allusion to the fact that the miracle is antitype of that performed by Elisha (2 Kings 4:38-44). Moreover, it is also probable that John introduces the notion of barley loaves to underline the poverty of human nourishment. Barley bread, food given to animals, was the bread of the poor. Hence, it stands in contrast to the bread which Jesus will give (vv. 26-59).

In answer to the difficulties presented by Philip and Andrew, Jesus simply tells the disciples to bid the crowd recline. Then, as we have already observed, Jesus performs an action which is reminiscent of the account of the institution of the Eucharist. John's account, in contrast to that of the Synoptics, adds eucharistic coloring to the narrative by picturing Jesus as personally distributing the bread to the crowd.

B. MIRACULOUS SUPERABUNDANCE (12-13)   There are other important differences between the accounts of the feeding miracle in John and in the Synoptics which bring out the fact that John understands it as a type of the Eucharist. The Synoptics relate that after the crowd had eaten, it gathered the fragments. According to John, Jesus tells the disciples to do this "in order that *nothing* be lost" (v. 12), and in verse 13 it is stated that the disciples carried out this order. The fact that the disciples are given the charge to gather up the remains emphasizes their value. As types of eucharistic food, they must be treated with reverence. Furthermore, it is explicitly said that the disciples filled twelve baskets with the fragments of the *five barley loaves* "left over" by those who had eaten (v. 13). It is the bread that matters. The Synoptics speak only of the gathering of the fragments, and Mark 6:43 adds that the remains of the fish were also collected.

The Synoptics recount the actual miracle in a series of main clauses: the actual eating, being filled, leaving remains. In John the references to the eating and being filled are placed in a subordinate clause: "But when they were filled . . ." (v. 12), which shows that John's construction is secondary. The "being filled" could only have been mentioned in passing if it had once figured in a main clause, for it was not the most natural thing in the world that so large a crowd would have been provided for with such a small quantity of food. The Synoptics, consequently, describe the miracle as consisting in the fact that all ate and were satisfied with a small amount of food which had been multiplied beyond their present needs. John, on the other hand, does not stress the subjective element of the eating and being satisfied. He emphasizes (1) the plentiful distribution by Jesus: Jesus distributed "as much as they wished" (v. 11); (2) the remains. In this way the miracle becomes a clear type of the *inexhaustible* bread (each one was given as much as he wished) and of the *imperishable* bread (the remains).

Especially noteworthy is John's emphasis on the remains. Although the Synoptics also stress the fact of the bountiful supply, John goes beyond this. The remains, which John gives us to understand are only the fragments of the five barley loaves, become a second miracle. The disciples are told to gather up the fragments in order that *"nothing* be lost" (and not "in order that they be not lost"). This statement calls attention to the value of the fragments as a type. Moreover, in the command of Jesus given to the disciples, the reference to the *remains* ("the fragments that *remain*") is superfluous and somewhat unnatural. In verse 13 the same stress on the *remains* is found. The somewhat ponderous statement that the disciples gathered up "the fragments of the five barley loaves which remained unto them that had eaten" would seem to indicate that John wishes to call special attention to the imperishable quality of the superfluous bread. It seems fair to say that John is pointing out that the bread, though eaten, remains and is even increased. It is imperishable, as the mention of the exact number of loaves reveals. If twelve baskets are filled with the "fragments of the five barley loaves which remained unto them that had eaten," then the loaves are not consumed and are even more numerous than before.

There is another argument which seems to indicate that John is consciously teaching that this bread is to be understood as incorruptible. Set in the context of the Exodus events, this miracle is, in John's eyes, antitype of the manna of the desert. But unlike the manna which was gathered only according to the needs of the people and which spoiled if too much were taken (Ex. 16:16-21), this surplus bread is *ordered* to be gathered. There is the implicit understanding that although gathered, it remains unspoiled. In the hands of Jesus the bread multiplies and remains. It is a type of the bread which Jesus will promise on the next day, a bread "which endures unto life everlasting, which the Son of Man will give you" (v. 27).

In the light of this explanation, the conversation between Jesus and the disciples concerning the meaning of the feeding miracle which is mentioned in Mark 8:13-21 (cf. Matt. 16:5-12) becomes understandable. We have already observed that Mark stresses the inability of the disciples to interpret the feeding miracle as a sign. It should be further noted that both Mark and Matthew stress only one aspect of the feeding miracle: *the remains*. In the conversation between Jesus and the disciples, no mention is made of the eating and being filled, though this was made a great deal of in the accounts of the actual miracle. Both Mark and Matthew note that the disciples' misunderstanding concerned their failure to recognize the miracle of the remains as a sign of the inexhaustible, imperishable bread.

The miraculous feeding of the 5,000 is not only a renewal of the prodigy of the desert but also a sign of the inexhaustible bread to be given by Christ: the word of revelation and the Eucharist. It signifies, as John is at pains to point out, the superabundance and permanence of the nourishment harvested by the twelve Apostles from the cross of Christ. In particular, John describes the miracle as a prophetic anticipation of the Lord's Supper. In the full light of the revelation of the Eucharist, John recognizes the feeding miracle as a type of the eucharistic banquet organized, directed, and served by Jesus. It is a type of that banquet which will reach beyond the hope of the Jews for the return of the material manna which fed their fathers in the desert.

C. Reaction of the Crowd and the Withdrawal of Jesus (14-15)

After the account of the miraculous feeding, John describes the reaction of the crowd. Convinced by the miracle that Jesus is the prophet to come, they attempt to make Him king. This Messianic enthusiasm is understandable. According to Jewish speculation of the time, the Messiah would come at the Passover and distribute the manna which had ceased to fall on the day when the Israelites entered the promised land. The crowd seems to have taken Jesus for the Messiah and the feeding miracle as a sign of the long-awaited return of the manna. The subsequent refusal of Jesus to accept the kingship indicates that the popular notion of the Messiah and His destiny is false. The true fate of the Messiah will be revealed in the course of the bread-of-life discourse: By refusing to accept the role of king at this period of His life, Jesus points to the fact that He must first be "given" for the life of the world (v. 52). The act of withdrawal heightens the mystery of Jesus.

II. *Miracle of the Walking on Water and Related Events* (16-25)

A. MIRACLE OF THE WALKING ON WATER (16-20)   This miracle, historically linked to the feeding miracle, is included here because of its significance for the theme of the chapter. Just as does the miracle of the loaves and fishes, John's account of the miracle of the walking on the water differs in minor details from that presented by the Synoptics. By means of some adjustments, the narrative is centered more on the person of Jesus. Many of the details found in the Synoptic versions are lacking in John: (1) The disciples are not constrained to get into the boat; (2) no mention is made of the quieting of the winds; (3) the act of adoration by the disciples is omitted; (4) no reference is made to Peter's dramatic attempt to walk on water. However, John alone notes that the boat had come "some twenty-five or thirty stadia" before the disciples saw Jesus walking on the troubled waters. This means that Jesus had traveled some three or four miles before encountering the disciples. The net effect of these changes is to reduce the role of the disciples to a minimum and to emphasize the magnitude of the miracle.

B. MIRACULOUS ARRIVAL AT THE SHORE (21)   When the disciples expressed their desire that Jesus get into the boat, a kind of second miracle occurred. In the Synoptic accounts, Jesus got into the boat, whereupon there took place a miraculous quieting of the winds (Mark 6:51; Matt. 14:32). The boat then sailed in calm water to the land (Mark 6:53; Matt. 14:34). John does not mention that Jesus got into the boat or that the wind ceased. Rather, he seems to indicate that the boat was in some mysterious way transported to land just as Jesus was about to get into it: "They desired therefore to take Him into the boat; and immediately the boat was at the land towards which they were going" (v. 21). The effect of this change is likewise to heighten the mystery of the person of Jesus whose presence and power transcend the laws which govern the conduct of ordinary men.

C. RECOGNITION BY THE CROWD OF THE MIRACLE (22-25)   John suggests, and clearly so, that the crowd understands that Jesus came across the lake in a miraculous manner. He goes out of his way to observe that the crowd noticed that there was *one* boat and "that Jesus had not gone into the boat with His disciples, but that His disciples had departed alone" (v. 22). At first glance it seems utterly superfluous to mention that the crowd noticed that Jesus had not got into the boat, when it was already stated in verse 15 that Jesus had fled from the crowd to the mountain. But John wishes to show that the crowd is quite aware of the situation. If, then, they do find Jesus on the other side of the lake on the next day, they will recognize that some miraculous event has taken place. This explains the question asked by the crowd when they actually confronted Jesus the following day: "Rabbi, when did You come here?" (v. 25). These people realize that some mysterious, supernatural event has taken place. Their surprise at finding Jesus on the opposite shore calls attention to the mystery of the person of Jesus and shows that the crowd should be prepared for the revelation which Jesus is about to make.

Function of miracles in the Fourth Gospel   At this point we should reflect for a moment on the function which miracles have in the Fourth Gospel. We have observed that the miracles of the multiplication of the loaves and fishes and the walking on water are recounted in view of the discourse which follows. They are the symbolic expressions of the bread-of-life discourse, and their full meaning will be known only after the discourse. For the present they focus attention on the mystery of the person of Jesus. Who is this man who gives imperishable bread in abundance, refuses the kingship of the world, and comes to His disciples and the crowd in a marvelous fashion?

This use of miracles in John 6 is in accordance with the special function of miracles in the Fourth Gospel, and which is distinguished from their function in the Synoptics. As are other revelations in John, the bread-of-life discourse is associated with miracles which are called *signs* (v. 26). The use of the word "sign" in this connection is not to indicate that the miracle is merely a proof of Jesus' divine power or mission. It refers to what Jesus is for men. Jesus raises Lazarus from the dead as a sign of what He is for all mankind: "I am the resurrection and the life" (11:25). Again, Jesus gives sight to the blind man as a sign that He is the light of the world: "I am the light of the world" (9:5). Each time Jesus reveals that He is, in a higher sense, precisely what He gives: the divine dispenser of light and life. This same pattern is found in John 6, when Jesus gives imperishable bread to the crowd as a sign that He is the "bread of life" (vv. 26-60).

III. *Discourse on the Bread of Life* (26-60)

GENERAL STYLE OF THE DISCOURSE   The discourse follows the easily identifiable Semitic style. In this type of exposition we do not encounter a modern, orderly treatment of ideas, each one of which is successively amplified to the full extent intended by the author. Rather, a number of connected topics are introduced in the initial stage. Next, one particular point is singled out for further development and the others are treated more briefly. Then, in turn, each of the other topics is amplified in sections which also shed light on the topics already treated or those to be singled out later for special attention. An author may, for example, introduce three associated concepts one after the other. Then in the subsequent development, each section of the composition will contain a fuller development of one idea with brief references to the other two. He may treat topic A extensively, then B and C briefly, in section one. In section two B will be amplified, and A and C will receive less attention. Next, in section three, C will be developed and B and A will receive passing mention. There is a constant returning to each of the topics originally introduced until each topic and its relation to the others have been fully developed. In each of the circular expositions all the concepts are found, but each concept is not equally developed in each circle. This style is reminiscent of the ebb and flow of the tide. It does not admit well-defined divisions.

Following this general style, John 6:27 presents a number of associated ideas which are then developed in the manner just described. The crowd is told that it should *work* for the *food which endures unto life everlasting,* which the *Son of Man will give.* The value of this nourishment is assured for the *Father* has *accredited the Son,* has set His seal on Him. In the rest of the discourse, one idea after the other is explained in a circular fashion until the meaning of the initial image of verse 27 is fully developed.

MODIFICATION OF THE GENERAL STYLE   John adds his own modification to this general style. The discourse takes the form of a dialogue divided into sections, which are in turn subdivided in the following way: (1) revelation of Jesus, (2) response of the audience, (3) further revelation of Jesus. In this form the response coming after the initial revelation manifests the lack of understanding of the audience but at the same time yields up the central theme of the revelation just given and points to a further revelation. This method is used in John 3 and 4 and brings out an important point which John is careful to make: the incapacity of human reason to penetrate the revelation of the Word. By this method John places *faith* at the center of the discussion.

A. REVELATION OF THE TRUE BREAD FROM HEAVEN (26-34)   1. *Revelation of Jesus concerning imperishable food which the Son of Man will give (26-27)*   The crowd had asked in verse 25: "Rabbi, when did You come here?" Jesus does not answer this question. He rebukes them for having stopped at the material aspect of the miracle of the loaves and fishes, of "having been filled," and for not having seen the *signs* (plural: the abundant distribution and the remains). Equivalently, Jesus is telling them that they sought Him because of the subordinate clause ("But when they were filled") and not because of the main clause of verse 12 which is concerned with the remains that filled twelve baskets.

To make His point, Jesus states in verse 27 that there is an imperishable food which men should work for and which the Son of Man will give. This food, of which the feeding miracle was a sign, will endure unto life everlasting. This is assured, says Jesus, since the Father has set His seal on the Son who gives it. In this revelation Jesus distinguishes implicitly between the promised food and the manna of the desert. Manna corrupted if too much were taken (Ex. 16:16-20); this food endures unto life everlasting. The imperishable food is also distinguished from the bread of the feeding miracle: It is food which the Son of Man *will give,* and it is food which is not obtainable without work.

From the beginning of the discourse the focus is on (1) the mystery of the Son of Man on whom the Father has set His seal and (2) the imperishable food which He will give, but not without the cooperation of the recipient.

It is noteworthy that from the outset Jesus is depicted as the Son of Man. This term *Bar Enash* does not of itself indicate a being above the stature of an ordinary human. Ezekiel the prophet is called "son of man" (Ezek. 2:1; 3:1, 4). It is true, moreover, that the Church Fathers had difficulty in understanding this term and often interpreted it as portraying the humble, suffering side of the Saviour. This interpretation which emphasizes the humanity of Christ is justifiable in some cases (Matt. 8:20; 11:19), but there are other cases for which it is insufficient. In these texts the title is linked to a glorious, transcendent destiny. Christ speaks of Himself as Son of Man when describing His Second Coming in triumph and glory (Mark 14:62; Matt. 26:64). Nor does Christ limit His role as Son of Man to the eschatological judgment. He declares Himself to be here and now this person of celestial origin endowed with supernatural power: "The Son of Man is Lord of the Sabbath" (Matt. 12:8; Mark 2:28) and has "authority on earth to forgive sins" (Matt. 9:6).

In John 6:27 we find the title "Son of Man" associated with imperishable food. It is the Son of Man who will give this food which endures unto life everlasting. Also, at the two other crucial phases of the discourse, reference is made to the Son of Man (vv. 54, 63). This appeal to the concept of the Son of Man at the most difficult stages of the discourse corresponds to the analogous movement of the dialogues with Nathaniel (1:51), Nicodemus (3:13), and the Jews of Jerusalem (5:27). On the question of Jesus' supernatural knowledge, the mysterious baptismal regeneration, and the power to give life and judge men, Christ appeals to the manifestation of the Son of Man elevated, glorified, and returned to His place of origin. The Ascension of Christ will make all these claims understandable, as well as the claims made in the discourse on the bread of life. The mystery of the Son of Man "ascended where He was before" (v. 63) will explain in great part the mysterious revelation which Jesus gives.

2. *Dialogue on works to be done* (28-31)   In response to Jesus' words, the audience asks how one must labor in order to do the works willed by God (v. 28). The crowd fastened onto the reference to imperishable food which Jesus promised to give, and they interpret this food to be the revelation of God's will. Jesus had also referred to the mystery of His own person as Son of Man, but this statement is left to one side.

Jesus answers the crowd by stating that the unique work willed by God is that men believe in the one sent by Him (v. 29). In this way He brings the discussion back to His person.

The audience now takes the hint and turns its attention to the person of Jesus. Why should they believe in Jesus? What are His credentials? They ask for a sign (vv. 30-31). They state that manna was given in the desert and quote Psalm 78:24 which testifies to this. The words "Bread from heaven he gave them to eat" are taken to refer to Moses. Moses gave the people manna in the desert through his intercession. What sign does Jesus perform to prove His powers of mediation? It is likely that the audience has in mind a return of the manna of the desert. We have already remarked that according to the Jewish speculation of the time, the Messiah would announce Himself through the bestowal of manna (cf. Chap-

ter One). This reference to Psalm 78:24, taken in connection with
the parallel passage in Mark 8:11, indicates that the audience is
equivalently saying: Give us *the* sign from heaven, the manna
which Moses gave in the desert. This will prove that You are God's
prophet.

3. *Further revelation about the nature of the imperishable food*
(32-33)   Jesus proceeds to give further revelation concerning the
imperishable food mentioned in verse 27. First, He rejects any relationship between the manna of the desert and the food which
He will give. Although the manna fell from the sky, it is not the
true bread from heaven which Jesus has promised to give and
which the Father gives in the first place (v. 32). The stress on the
giving by the Father underlines the Father's pre-eminent place in
the work of salvation. If the Son gives anything it is because the
Father has already given it.

Continuing the contrast between manna and the "bread of God,"
Jesus states that the latter gives *life to the world* (v. 33). The manna
had no such power, as Jesus will shortly observe: "Your fathers ate
the manna in the desert, and have died" (v. 49).

4. *Request of the audience for the imperishable bread* (34)   The
mysterious words of Jesus induce the audience to request: "Lord
give us always this bread." Jesus will interpret the meaning of *always* in the next verse.

B. REVELATION THAT THE BREAD OF HEAVEN IS THE INCARNATE SON
WHO GIVES REVELATION (35-47)   1. *Revelation of Jesus that He is
the bearer of revelation and the Incarnate Son of the Father* (35-40)
In response to the petition of the audience, Jesus declares that He
is the bread of life given by the Father in the sense that "He who
comes to me shall not hunger, and he who believes in me shall never
thirst" (v. 35). Here "bread of life" is used as a metaphor. "To eat
bread" can mean "to receive doctrine" according to Jewish usage
(Prov. 9:5). Christ identifies Himself with His doctrine. He equivalently says: "My doctrine will be spiritual nourishment for you."

In saying that "he who believes in Me shall *never* thirst," Jesus interprets the "always" of verse 34 to mean that He will never withdraw Himself from those who have faith in Him.

Although the context of verse 35 concerns only the eating of bread, the question of drinking is introduced. This reference may be deliberately ambiguous and may allude to the eating and drinking of the eucharistic Christ who, in the sacramental food and drink, satisfies spiritual hunger and thirst.

Having introduced the topic of belief in the revelation which He brings, Jesus now returns to the mystery of His person and asserts that though the hearers *see* Him they do not believe (v. 36). The reason for their disbelief lies in the fact that the Father has not given them the gift of faith (v. 37). All who receive faith come to Jesus and He receives them. The basis for the harmony between Jesus and the Father is explained: Jesus has "come down from heaven" to do the will of the Father who sent Him (v. 38). It is the will of the Father that Jesus should not lose anyone who has been given to Him and that He should raise all these chosen ones on the last day (v. 39).

Explaining more fully the last statement, Jesus says that it is the will of the Father that those to whom He has given the grace to behold the Son and believe in Him shall have everlasting life and be raised up by Jesus on the last day (v. 40). The effect of faith in Christ is salvation: everlasting life and the glorious resurrection of the body. Thus, Jesus brings out the truth that the Father attracts men through the Son, the unique mediator. The Father gives the true bread: Christ; and Christ gives the revelation of the Father. The Father also gives the grace of faith by which men are enabled to receive Christ's doctrine.

2. *Objection of the Jews to the mystery of the Incarnation* (41-42)
The Jews murmur against Jesus because He says: "I am the bread that has come down from heaven" (v. 41). This quotation which the Jews attribute to Jesus disengages the central affirmation of verses 35-40: the heavenly origin of Jesus. They cannot accept this claim and "murmur" as their fathers murmured in the desert against the manna which they no longer desired (Num. 11). Like

their fathers, the Jews do not wish to accept Jesus, whom the Father gives, as the bread of life.

The subsequent question put by the Jews confirms the fact that they object to Jesus' claim to celestial origin: "Is this not Jesus the son of Joseph, whose father and mother we know? How, then, does He say, 'I have come down from heaven?'" (v. 42). They are scandalized. They do not "behold the Son and believe in Him" (v. 40); they see only the son of Joseph. The question is a rhetorical one intended as ridicule. The answer is given in the question itself. Jesus cannot be of celestial origin for He is the son of Joseph. It is an example of "judging according to the flesh" which Jesus condemns elsewhere in a similar context (John 8:15; cf. 7:24).

3. *Revelation by Jesus of the mystery of faith* (43-47)   Jesus answers the Jews by telling them not to "murmur" and thus insinuates that they are as sceptical as their fathers (v. 43). He goes on to explain the reason why they do not accept His claim to be the Incarnate Son of God. Only he to whom the Father has given the grace of faith, that is, who has listened to the Father and learned, comes to Jesus (vv. 44-45). On this matter, Jesus asserts, He has authority to speak because "He has seen the Father" (v. 46).

The section closes with a solemn affirmation of the effect of faith in Jesus. In verse 44 Jesus had promised a glorious resurrection for those who have faith in Him. Now he states that there is an effect attributable to faith here and now: "Amen, amen, I say to you, he who believes in Me has life everlasting" (v. 47). The effect of faith is the possession of eternal life here and now.

C. REVELATION THAT THE BREAD OF HEAVEN IS THE INCARNATE SON IN HIS EUCHARISTIC PRESENCE (48-60)   This section, just as the previous one, develops the revelation begun in the first section. Both sections begin with the same topic sentence: "I am the bread of life." There is an analogous development. In both cases the revelation of Jesus is met with a strong objection from the Jews who are singled out from among the crowd. In both cases the objection leads to a fuller explanation of a mystery. But there is an evolution in thought which is indicated by the fact that the key words of verses 35-47, *to come to Me / to believe in Me,* are replaced by *to give / to eat and drink.* Thus, we finally come to the midrashic exegesis of the word "eat" of Psalm 78:24, which has been neglected up to now.

1. *Revelation of Jesus that the eating of the living flesh of the sacrificed Christ gives eternal life* (48-52)   Up to now Jesus has not referred explicitly to the statement of the Jews made in verse 31: "Our fathers ate manna in the desert." At this point He quotes their remark and adds that those who ate the manna died (v. 49). In contrast to this material food, there is a "bread of life" (v. 48), a "bread that comes down from heaven, so that if anyone eat of it he will not die" (v. 50). This bread is Jesus Himself: "I am the living bread that has come down from heaven" (v. 51).

Previously in verse 33 Jesus spoke of the bread of God which comes down from heaven and gives life to the world, and He identified Himself with this bread (v. 35). But in what sense is He bread? In the subsequent development to verse 47, Jesus identifies Himself with His doctrine. He is the bread of life in the sense that He transmits saving revelation which, if assimilated by faith, gives eternal life. However in verses 48-52 a new mode of participation in Christ is revealed. It is no longer a question of participation in the word of revelation by believing, but of participation in the Incarnate Word Himself by eating: "If anyone eat of this bread he shall live forever; and the bread that I will give is My flesh for the life of the world" (v. 52).

Up to this point in the discourse we have learned that the Father gives the Incarnate Son to the world, and that the Son gives the revelation of the Father. Now Jesus reveals that He gives Himself for the life of the world, and that the effect of participating in His flesh by eating is life everlasting. The meaning of verse 52b is clear from the context, which concerns a gift men participate in by "eating." It signifies: The bread I will give *men* is My flesh for the life of the world. The word "give" (*didōmi*) in verse 52b does not refer to the offering which Christ makes of Himself to the Father but to the bestowal of Himself on men. In other places in the Fourth Gospel we find statements which refer to the self-giving of

Jesus to the Father for the salvation of men. In none of these cases is the offering of Jesus expressed by *didōmi*. This word is used by John to indicate the bestowal of the redemptive gifts on men. However, implicitly Jesus refers to His redemptive mediation. His flesh has redemptive value because it is offered as an acceptable sacrifice to the Father. This sacrificial aspect will be brought out more prominently in verses 54-57 through the introduction of the term "blood."

A new gift is promised to men. Besides revelation mankind will be given the "living" flesh of the redeeming mediator. If a man "eat" this flesh he will receive eternal life. What are we to understand by this statement? In view of the previous section (vv. 35-47), it is conceivable that Jesus could have meant that men must believe in His redemptive mediation: the life-bestowing sacrifice of Christ's humanity. The result of this belief would be the reception of the fruits of the cross: eternal life. In this case "flesh" would be identified with sacrificial death. To eat flesh would mean to believe in the sacrificial mediation of Christ, just as in the previous section the reception of the bread of life meant the reception of the doctrine which Christ preached. However, there are indications that more is meant than participation by an act of faith. The mode of participation is characterized as an "eating," and there are no indications that this action is to be identified with an act of faith. In the previous section it was explicitly stated that men must have a living faith in the revelation which Jesus brings. Hence, a fruitful "eating" involves an act of faith. Nevertheless, this concept turns the discourse in another direction. We are already on the sacramental plane. This is confirmed by the resemblance between verse 52b and the Lukan and Pauline versions of the words of institution spoken over the bread, and by the fact that verses 48-52 portray Jesus as distributing bread, His flesh, at a banquet. Further explanation will be needed, but the discourse already points toward the Eucharist.

2. *Objection of the Jews* (53)   In verse 42 the Jews objected to the claim of heavenly origin, and so they rejected Jesus' authority to teach them. The new notion of "eating" which Jesus inserts into

the web of the discourse also attracts their attention. They recognize it as a key word that involves more than belief in Jesus' teaching. But what can it mean? "How can this man give us His flesh to eat?" Christ had not made this exact statement, but the Jews rightly disengage it as the central affirmation of verses 48-52.

This question of the Jews is different in tenor from the one asked in verse 42. It concerns the practicality of Jesus' remark. How can this assertion of Jesus be applied in the concrete? The fact that the Jews *disputed violently (emachonto)* among themselves seems to indicate that this question is a sincere one. Also, no reason is given for the rejection of the statement made by Jesus as was done in verse 42.

Some have thought that the Jews are equivalently asking: How can this man be the universal mediator? This interpretation is unacceptable, for if it were so then the Jews should have fixed on the final remark made by Christ: ". . . and the bread that I will give is My flesh for the life of the world." But the Jews combine the totality of the statements made by Jesus and stress the concept of *eating*. Their question is unequivocal and continues on the sacramental plane: What does this man mean by saying that He can give us His flesh to eat?

3. *Further revelation of the eucharistic mystery: the necessity of eating the eucharistic flesh and blood and the effects of sacramental communion* (54-60)   Having heard the discussion of the Jews, Jesus confirms what He has already said. He assures His audience that men must eat His flesh and drink His blood if they will have life. Three times Jesus repeats the assertion that His flesh must be eaten and His blood drunk (vv. 54, 55, 57), and He adds for good measure that "My flesh is food indeed, and My blood is drink indeed" (v. 56). The eating of Christ's flesh is further qualified as meaning "to eat Me" (v. 58).

The language used by Christ is startling, but made acceptable by the insertion of the concept of the Son of Man. The Jews had asked: "How can this *man* give us His flesh to eat?" Jesus answers by saying that men must eat "the flesh of the Son of Man" (v. 54).

It is the mystery of the Son of Man that will make this intelligible. The eucharistic sense of the passage is inescapable. The expressions "to eat My flesh" and "to drink My blood" are unmistakable references to the double blessing of the bread and wine at the Last Supper. The repetition of the word "truly [indeed]" in verse 56 is used to prevent any watering down of the sacramental realism: Christ's flesh and blood are truly (*alēthēs*) nourishment. Some scholars have thought that John uses a special word for "to eat" (*trōgein*) to stress sacramental realism (vv. 55, 57, 58, 59). In profane Greek, this is a strong word which means to gnaw, nibble, or munch. However, it would seem best to say that no special emphasis is intended by this word. In the Fourth Gospel *esthion*, the usual supplement for the defective aorist *phagein* (to eat) in the present tense is not found. Thus, where the LXX version of Psalm 41:9 uses *esthion*, John uses *trōgōn* (John 13:18). Because of this more general use of *trōgōn* by John, we cannot argue that it is employed for special emphasis in our pericope. At any rate sacramental realism is assured especially by the concept of *drinking blood*. This notion also points out that it is the body-given-for-many, the sacrificed body, which must be eaten.

The effect of eating and drinking the sacrificed body and blood of the Son of Man is explained in this passage. We have already seen that the effect of belief in the revelation which Jesus brings is eternal life as a present possession and the assurance of a glorious resurrection (vv. 35-47). The same effect upon eating the flesh of the Saviour of the world is noted in verses 48-52 and is repeated in verse 55: "He who eats My flesh and drinks My blood has life everlasting and I will raise him up on the last day." Not content with this general statement, Jesus goes on to develop the meaning of the life which is given through the Eucharist to the communicant who receives it with living faith.

From the viewpoint of this discourse, to say that the Eucharist gives *life everlasting* is the same thing as saying: "He who eats My flesh, and drinks My blood, abides in Me and I in him" (v. 57). It is a life which the communicants have in common with Christ, as the words "abides in Me and I in him" indicate. This formula, peculiar to the Johannine writings (John 15:4-7; 17:21-26; 1 John 2:24; 3:24; 4:16), describes what might be called a reciprocal interaction and interpenetration, a reciprocal indwelling. Furthermore, it concerns something more than a merely moral relationship of love, as the word "in" (*en*) suggests. It refers to an ontological association of life. It touches being itself. But this indwelling does not submerge the personality of either party of the relationship. It is a personal association in which each of the partners retains his own identity: "*he* in Me and *I* in him." Nor is this encounter described as a passing experience, a thing of the moment. It is stamped as an "abiding" possession: a redeeming or grace-reality.

The nature of this life shared by the communicant and Christ is described more fully in the following verse: "As the living Father has sent Me, and as I live because of the Father, so he who eats Me, he also shall live because of Me" (v. 58). Here the prototype and foundation of the indwelling of the believing communicant with Christ is seen as the Divine Circumincession. The partaking of the Eucharist gives to the believer a share in the life which Jesus receives from the Father. Jesus who was sent from the Father—a sending which is the image of the inner-Trinitarian procession of the Son from the Father—also lives through the "living Father" who is the author of all life and who gives it to the Son from all eternity (John 17:5).

This divine life is not twofold; that is, it is not in the Father and separately in the Son. The Son and the Father are *one* as Jesus points out in the High Priestly prayer (John 17:20-23). Father and Son have a unity of life, though the Father possesses it as one who begets and the Son as one who is begotten. It is this life which is given to the believing recipient of the Eucharist.

Briefly, the reception of the Eucharist involves a personal encounter with the Son of Man sacrificed for the redemption of the world. This encounter effects a reception of the fruit of the redemptive work: a reciprocal indwelling of the believer and Christ, which of its very nature involves an intimate association with the Father. The "abiding" in the Son implies a share in the "abiding" of the Son in the Father and the Father in the Son in union with the Holy Spirit: a share in the Trinitarian life.

Historical note   This discourse closes with the observation that "These things He said when teaching in the synagogue at Capharnaum" (v. 60). Hence, this dialogue took place either Friday night or Saturday morning when the Jews gathered for the weekly service. This fact would place the multiplication of the loaves and fishes on Thursday. Perhaps this observation of John is another conscious effort to link the feeding miracle with the Eucharist, the institution of which would take place on Thursday of the Passover week one year later.

IV. *Reaction of the Disciples and Related Events* (61-72)

A. Objection of the Disciples (61)   The relation of the Eucharist to the faith is now touched on in a very concrete way. Many of the disciples are scandalized at the words of Jesus. Their reaction is recorded: "Many of His disciples therefore, when they heard this, said, 'This is a hard saying. Who can listen to it?'" (v. 61). Faced with a mystery which could not be understood by reason alone, but which ought to be accepted in faith, many of Christ's followers turned away. This observation of John once again brings faith to the foreground. Without the condition of believing surrender, the mystery of the Incarnation, Christ's teaching and sacrificial mediation, and the Eucharist must be rejected, for the human intellect left to itself cannot comprehend them.

B. Revelation of the Mediatorial Power of the Glorified Son of Man and the Necessity of the Grace of Faith (62-66) Aware of the murmuring of some of the disciples, Jesus asks: "Does this scandalize you? What if you should see the Son of Man ascending where He was before?" (62-63). Up to this time Jesus has revealed the Eucharist in two of its basic dimensions: Incarnation and redemptive sacrifice. In the discourse on the bread of life, Jesus had first stressed the necessity of belief in the revelation which He gives, basing His authority on His position as Incarnate Son who has seen the Father. He then revealed the necessity of eating and drinking the flesh and blood which He assumed and which is offered in sacrifice for mankind. In nourishing himself on the Eucharist, the believer adheres to the Incarnate Son of God sacrificed for men and thus communicates in the fruits of redemption: eternal life and the glorious resurrection of the body.

But the enigma remains: How can Jesus in the condition of His mortal body (1) pretend to vivify men with eternal life, (2) raise them from the dead on the last day, (3) give Himself as food? Jesus had already hinted at the solution by referring to Himself as Son of Man in the eucharistic context. Now He explains further. The exact meaning of verse 63 is disputed because it is incomplete. The sentence lacks an apodasis. The apodasis could be: "Will you still be scandalized?" or, "Will you then desist from taking scandal?" In any case, Jesus refers to His glorious Ascension, apparently as an attempt to help the disciples understand the mystery of the Eucharist. In other words, the Son of Man in His glorified state will remove the triple enigma. He will be capable of communicating divine life, of raising the believers in triumph on the last day, of giving Himself as spiritual food.

The disciples are invited to examine the Eucharist in conjunction with the mystery of the Ascension, which according to the Fourth Gospel is the condition for the sending of the Spirit (John 7:39). Christ thus implies that He does not require a material eating of His flesh and a material drinking of His blood, but a spiritual eating and drinking of the glorified body and blood which are not subject to the same conditions to which His humanity was subject during His earthly sojourn.

In the following verse, verse 64, Jesus says: "It is the spirit that gives life; the flesh profits nothing." This statement can refer to both the previous verse and to the sentence which follows. As explanation of the question asked in verse 63, it would mean: Christ in the condition of His mortal body on earth does not give eternal life, but He will do so as Son of Man, spiritualized through His glorification. In conjunction with the sentence which follows, it must be understood as the application of the well-known biblical concept of the fragility of the flesh and the vivifying power of the spirit to Jesus' teaching (cf. John 3:6). Thus verse 64b would mean: "The words I have spoken to you are [vivified by the] Spirit and [thus become bearers of] life."

Returning to the subject of His teaching and its life-giving power (cf. vv. 35-47), Jesus introduces again the question of belief. Not all have the gift of faith: "But there are some among you who do not believe" (v. 65). This mystery of unbelief provokes a comment by John: "For Jesus knew from the beginning who they were who did not believe, and who it was who should betray Him" (v. 65). The mystery of predestination is brought to the foreground. In the moment of final decision, the mystery of human liberty which refuses the invitation of God is situated in the more profound mystery of election by the Father.

There follows a statement by Jesus on the divine initiative underlying the faith similar to that given in verses 37 and 44: "No one can come to Me unless he is enabled to do so by My Father" (v. 66).

C. OPTION OF THE DISCIPLES (67-70)   The foregoing revelation brings on a crisis in the ministry of Jesus: "From this time many of His disciples turned back and no longer went about with Him" (v. 67). Men cannot remain indifferent to the revelation of Christ. They must choose for or against Him. Those who reject Christ are contrasted with those who accept His words in faith. After the defection of many of His followers, Christ challenges the Twelve: "Do you also wish to go away?" (v. 68). Peter answers for the rest with a profession of faith in the belief that Jesus gives the revelation of the Father and is the Son of God: "Thou hast the words of everlasting life, and we have come to believe and to know that Thou art the Christ, the Holy One of God" (vv. 69-70).

D. PROPHECY OF JUDAS' BETRAYAL (71-72)   But even within the Twelve the mystery of election clashes with the mystery of human liberty. Christ has chosen the Twelve and yet one will reject Him: "Have I not chosen you, the Twelve? Yet one of you is a devil" (v. 71). Commenting on this, John leaves no doubt as to whom Jesus was referring: "Now He was speaking of Judas Iscariot, the son of Simon; for he it was, though one of the Twelve, who was to betray Him" (v. 72). This is the second reference to the betrayal by Judas (cf. v. 65) and serves to point out that free cooperation is required with the gift of faith. It also provides a link with the Last Supper. These references to Judas recall the night when Christ will give the promised flesh and blood to the Apostles and Judas will betray Him to His enemies. John has deliberately opened this chapter with an oblique reference to the Last Supper (v. 4), and now he closes it with a similar reference.

Summa Summarum

John 6:1-72 presents a number of truths of Christian revelation and relates them to the Eucharist. The teaching of this chapter may be outlined as follows:

I. *Christ is the unique mediator of the new covenant.*
  A. He is the representative of the Father (27, 32, 37, 39, 40, 44, 46, 58, 66).
  B. He is the Incarnate Son of the Father (32, 33, 38, 40, 41, 42, 51, 63, 70).
  C. He establishes the new and eternal covenant:
   1. As the new Moses He feeds the people (1-13).
   2. He is called the prophet (14).
   3. He gives the new manna (27).
   4. He is the new manna (35, 41, 48, 51-59).
   5. He establishes the new covenant by sacrificial death (52).
  D. He brings the new covenant to completion with the Ascension (63).
  E. Mediation of the glorified Christ implies the sending of the Spirit (63-64; cf. 7:39; 14:26).

II. *There are consequences of the unique mediation of Christ.*
  A. Faith in the words of Jesus is necessary (29, 35, 40, 47, 65, 69-70).
  B. Salvation is obtained only through Jesus (27, 29, 33, 35, 39, 40, 44, 47, 50-59, 64, 66, 69-70).
  C. Salvation of the world obtained only through the sacrificial death of Jesus (52).
  D. The reception of the eucharistic Christ is necessary for salvation (54-59).

III. *There are effects of participation in Christ's redemptive work by faith and the Eucharist.*
  A. There is eternal life (27, 40, 47, 55, 59).
   1. Eternal life is a present possession (47, 55).
   2. Eternal life consists in a reciprocal interaction and interpenetration of Christ and the believer (57).

3. Eternal life is a share in the Trinitarian life (58).
   B. Resurrection of the body in glory results (39, 40, 44, 55).
IV. *There are requisites for salvation.*
   A. Predestination is necessary (37, 39, 65).
   B. Grace for good works is necessary (44, 66).
   C. Free cooperation of the individual with grace is necessary (36, 65, 67-70).

In the course of this development, the Eucharist emerges as a sacramental entity which is dependent for its efficacy on the three major mysteries of Christ's life: Incarnation, redemptive sacrifice, Resurrection-Ascension. It is the sacrament of the flesh and blood (Incarnation) of the Son of Man (Resurrection-Ascension) who offers Himself as a sacrifice for the salvation of the world (redemptive sacrifice). Being the re-presentation of the unique mediator and His redemptive work, it is necessary for salvation. It bestows eternal life and the pledge of a glorious resurrection on those who, drawn by the grace of faith, freely receive it.

Although faith is necessary for salvation and gives eternal life, the response of the believer to Christ is not to remain on the invisible plane. There is a visible affirmation of faith which is required: baptism and the Eucharist. The visible encounter with the redeemer sacramentally present in the "daily bread" of the Eucharist heralds a fruitful spiritual meeting between man and the Son of Man: It effects an "abiding" in the Trinitarian life which the Son receives from the Father.

One final remark is in order concerning the "abiding" in Christ effected through the Eucharist. The militant Christian retains eternal life as an eschatological possession. Always under the sign of *pas encore,* the Christian should realize with fear and trembling that eternal life can be lost. Thus, the "abiding" takes the form of an admonition. Though this aspect is not brought out in John 6, it is discussed in 1 John 2:28: "And now, dear children, abide in Him, so that when He appears we may have confidence, and may not shrink ashamed from Him at His coming" (cf. 1 John 3:24; 4:15-16).

In this chapter John has stressed the implications of the Eucharist for the individual. The social aspect of the Eucharist, a particular concern of St. Paul, is not discussed. However, many commentators have pointed out that the parable of the vine and branches in John 15:1ff. bears a close resemblance to John 6 and brings out the social aspect of the Eucharist. In this passage Jesus describes Himself as a grapevine and His disciples as the branches and draws the conclusion that "He who abides in Me, and I in him, he bears much fruit" (v. 5). The use of the plural in verse 4— "You abide in Me, and I in you"—shows that the abiding involves a community relationship between Christ and all His followers. All must abide in Christ, the basis of Christian existence, and this abiding effects a union among all the members of Christ. The symbol of the vine would seem to have eucharistic implications. The abiding of which Christ speaks is effected not only by faith and baptism but also by the reception of the eucharistic Christ, the "true vine."

The grace of intimate union of the disciples among themselves was, as John is careful to point out, the special object of Jesus' prayer at the Last Supper: ". . . that all may be one, even as Thou, Father, in Me and I in Thee; that they also may be in Us, that the world may believe that Thou hast sent Me" (John 17: 22). This prayer has great consequences for the unity demanded of Christians: (1) It is a union that should be analogous to that possessed by Father and Son: "that all may be one, even as Thou, Father, in Me and I in Thee." (2) It is a union of all in Christ and the Father: "That they also may be one in Us." (3) It is an intimate spiritual union that should manifest itself visibly: "that the world may believe."

Not only did Christ address this efficacious prayer to the Father at the Last Supper, but at the same time He gave the means to effect every petition of this prayer. The Eucharist unites men to Christ and in Christ with the Father in the intimate sharing of the Trinitarian life (John 6:57-58). At the same time, it effects an intimate spiritual union of the believers with one another in Christ (John 15:1ff.). But the Eucharist is also the efficacious *sign* par excellence of the union of all men in Christ. The same eucharistic bread and wine, received at a common table, signifies the union of the communicants among themselves in Christ. It is thus the most important sacrament given to the world that it may *see* the unity of men in Christ and consequently *believe* "that Thou hast sent Me."

AN HISTORICAL PROBLEM

The eucharistic interpretation of John 6:52-59 should be beyond dispute. Nevertheless, we are faced with the following problem: How could the Jews and disciples have understood the Eucharist well enough for Christ to have made this mystery the subject of a decision to accept or reject Him? The Jews and disciples were able to comprehend, to some extent, Christ's claim to be mediator after the manner of Moses. But without further explanation, the words "to eat My flesh" and "to drink My blood" would not have been understood at the time of the discourse except as a sacrilegious way of expressing the need for participation *by faith* in Christ's work of mediation. Even the theme of redemptive sacrifice, introduced into the eucharistic discourse properly so called, was not a familiar theme of contemporary Messianic teaching and would have required more than the passing reference it receives in the pericope.

It is conceivable that in the historical bread-of-life discourse Jesus developed these themes more fully. John would be merely reporting the substance of the discourse in outline form. On the other hand, is it not possible that the concepts of redemptive sacrifice and the Eucharist were introduced into the discourse by the author of the Fourth Gospel who, in light of the revelation of the Last Supper and the cross, saw the full implications of the historical bread-of-life discourse? Is it not possible that John is simply making explicit what Jesus implied by referring to Himself as the "bread of life"?

In the past the majority of Catholic exegetes and theologians took for granted that the whole bread-of-life discourse was given at Capharnaum. Today many feel that this interpretation is too simplified. It has long since been recognized that John does not intend to present a simple narrative of historical facts as one who writes a newspaper account of a speech given on a particular occasion. Rather, as any good historian, he interprets the significance of the historical events of Christ's life. If he has made the miracle of the multiplication of the loaves and fishes appear as a type of the Last Supper (that is, a eucharistic banquet organized and directed by Jesus), is it not possible, and indeed probable, that he used a similar technique in the bread-of-life discourse? A priori it seems that we would have to accept the possibility in view of John's general style and the difficulty involved in interpreting the passage in such a way that the Eucharist would be made the subject of the option for or against Christ this early in His public ministry.

The theory which proposes that verses 52-59 are an interpretation of the historical bread-of-life discourse is based on the modern understanding of the processes which played a part in the composition of the Gospels. This view begins with the presupposition that the Gospels contain the narrative of historical events, which were communicated to later generations mainly through oral tradition and which were recorded by the Evangelists for a special purpose. Further study of the oral tradition has revealed that only certain incidents were chosen from Jesus' life because of their special importance and aptness for preaching (*kerygma*), didactic instruction (*catechesis*), and liturgy. Likewise, it has been shown that the "living usage" called for adaptation in presentation. Sometimes the style of the narrative would be changed from a more primitive form to meet the exigencies of a particular situation, for example, the liturgical forms of the words of institution of the Eucharist. Sometimes the full significance of a particular event, known only in the light of the complete revelation, would be made explicit although it was not clear to the eyewitnesses at the time of the historical occurrence itself (for example, Mark 15:39).

Finally, it has been demonstrated that the oral tradition itself is altered when it passes into the written Gospels. The authors arranged the material in accordance with the special purpose or theme of the Gospel. In this way new light is thrown on the events of Christ's life. By the presentation of certain details, by the use of various literary devices, the historical events of Christ's life, a part of the natural history of mankind, are shown to have their most profound meaning on the level of salvation history.[1]

---

[1] The recent instruction of the Pontifical Biblical Commission, *Instructio de historica Evangeliorum veritate* [official English version to be found in *Catholic*

Applying this understanding of the prehistory of the Gospel material to the problem at hand, it seems fair to say that an adequate interpretation of John 6 should take into account the various influences which have played a part in its formation (History, *Sitz im Leben, Sitz im Evangelion*). On the historical level, we should bear in mind (1) the mentality of the Jews and disciples, (2) the stage of knowledge of the new revelation which they had attained, (3) the teaching methods of Jesus. On the level of the life of the primitive Church (*Sitz im Leben*), we should recall that the bread-of-life discourse would have meant much to Christians whose cultic life revolved around the heritage which they had received from the Last Supper. On the level of the written Gospel (*Sitz im Evangelion*), we should bear in mind that John wrote the sixth chapter after the Last Supper and filled it with eucharistic symbolism as a means of instructing the faithful about the profound meaning of the Eucharist in relation to the whole economy of redemption.

In the past, insufficient attention was devoted to the prehistory of the Gospel material, and as a result, various interpretations of the origin of the bread-of-life discourse concentrated on separate levels of existence. Consequently, the resolutions attained have not been satisfactory. By far the most traditional approach has been to concentrate on the historical setting exclusively, admit the literary unity of the chapter, and accept the bread-of-life discourse as the *quasi ipsissima verba Christi*. Beginning from this general viewpoint, several interpretations of verses 52-59 have gained wide acceptance. A traditional Catholic position is that the Jews and disciples understood Christ to speak of some sort of sacramental communion between Himself and believers. A traditional Protestant interpretation maintains that the Jews and disciples understood this passage to refer to the necessity of faith in the redeemer, and that Christ intended it in this way only. M. J. Lagrange theorizes that this section was heard by the disciples alone and not by the Jews.

Biblical Quarterly, Vol. 26 (July 1964), 305-12] admits, for the first time in any of its official communications, the distinction of the three stages of tradition in the Gospel material which has been the fruit of a form-critical study of the Gospels For an excellent commentary on this *Instructio*, see J. A. Fitzmyer, S.J., "The Biblical Commission's Instruction on the Historical Truth of the Gospels," *Theological Studies*, Vol. 25 (September 1964), 386-408.

This revelation was given later on in the ministry of Jesus when the disciples were better prepared to receive it.

The traditional Catholic interpretation remains possible but rather difficult in view of Jesus' teaching methods. To have made the Eucharist the object of a decisive option for or against Him so early in His ministry seems unlikely. The traditional Protestant interpretation cannot be accepted even as a possibility in view of the overwhelming evidence in favor of the eucharistic interpretation of this chapter. The opinion of Lagrange, finally, is not supported by the context. Taken as *an historical discourse,* verses 52-59 are an answer to an objection of the Jews and are addressed to the Jews and disciples.

Another type of interpretation, more popular today, concentrates on the immediate milieu in which the chapter originated, accepts the literary unity of the passage, and does not discuss whether or not verses 52-59 are to be understood as the *quasi ipsissima verba Christi.* According to advocates of this opinion, the passage refers to the Eucharist. What the Jews understood at Capharnaum is not treated because the historical setting is ignored. However, since the historical background of the discourse is assured (cf. section "Preliminary Observations," of this chapter), an adequate treatment of the pericope requires that it be taken into consideration.

There is another type of solution which solves the difficulty by denying the literary unity of the chapter and excising verses 52-59 as the product of a late Christian interpolation credited to an ecclesiastical redactor. According to R. Bultmann, and more recently G. Bornkamm, the bread-of-life discourse of the original Gospel of John discussed only the question of *faith.* The later addition of the eucharistic text is judged to be contrary to the theological perspective of the Fourth Gospel. Although this solution may do away with one problem, it creates more serious ones. The literary unity of this chapter is assured. Furthermore, the assertion that the sacramental teaching so often encountered in the Fourth Gospel is contrary to the theological outlook of the original text is completely unwarranted.

Considering the criticisms of the preceding theories, it would appear that a solution to the origin of the bread-of-life discourse as it is presented in John 6 must take into account, not only the literary unity of the chapter, but also the various levels of existence of the recorded material. Xavier Léon-Dufour, S.J. has presented a rather attractive interpretation. He takes into account the historical setting and the milieu in which the Gospel was written, while at the same time maintaining that the discourse reflects faithfully the actual words used by Jesus. According to him, verse 52b refers to the sacrificial death of Jesus and to the Eucharist. The former understanding would have been grasped by the audience which heard the historical bread-of-life discourse, and the readers of the Gospel would recognize the eucharistic reference. Léon-Dufour maintains that verses 53-59 should be interpreted in the same manner. At the time of the historical discourse, the words "to eat My flesh / to drink My blood" would be thought by the hearers to signify adhesion to the entire person of Christ the redeemer. He notes that verse 58 states that ". . . he who eats Me, he also shall live because of Me." Thus *flesh* and *blood* are equivalent to *Me* (and equal Jesus' person).

In particular Léon-Dufour doubts that the words "to drink My blood" would have been understood by the audience as an invitation to a sacramental drinking. He argues that this notion was foreign to the Jewish mentality: In Jewish rites the blood was poured out, not drunk. The hearers would understand Jesus to be referring to the fruits of His sacrifice. They would see in Jesus' words a call to find life by faith in His person and redemptive sacrifice. With the full revelation of the economy of salvation in their possession, the readers of the Fourth Gospel would perceive that Jesus had also meant the Eucharist: that by the sacramental participation in the Eucharist, the Christian actually partakes of the fruits of the redemptive sacrifice.

Following along the same pattern, Léon-Dufour interprets the option of verses 61ff. as revolving about the question of the unique mediation of Jesus. Jesus crowns His discourse by revealing that He exercises an absolute and eternal mediation. His sacrificed flesh will mount to heaven in a glorious Ascension and continue to vivify men. The hearers of the discourse understood that they were called upon to accept the perpetual mediation of Jesus as a matter of faith; the readers of the Gospel, on the other hand, understood that they received the glorified Son of Man in the Eucharist.

Although Léon-Dufour's solution has merit, it contains a fatal flaw. It appears utterly impossible to interpret verses 52-59 in a nonsacramental sense. It would have been most strange for Jesus to have used this language, especially the phrase "to drink blood," as an invitation to His hearers to find life in His person and redemptive sacrifice. Unprepared for this expression, the Jews would have found it sacrilegious. What possible purpose could it have served unless Jesus were revealing the Eucharist and expected His hearers to understand Him in that way?

There is also another difficulty with Léon-Dufour's analysis. He holds that the option of the Jews and disciples centered on the belief in Christ's mediation through sacrificial death. But if Léon-Dufour conjectures that the Jews and disciples could not have understood the Eucharist at Capharnaum, why should he suppose that they could have understood the notion of a suffering Messiah mediating salvation through His death? Although traces of the concept of the suffering Messiah may be found in Jewish tradition, this concept was not a familiar one to the Jews of the first century. Hence, it is just as surprising that it was made the subject of the option for or against Christ at this stage of His public ministry.

Léon-Dufour has proceeded in the right direction, but he has not gone far enough. On the basis of his own methodology, it is rather surprising that he did not take the final step which involves a consideration of the possibility that the words attributed to Jesus by John may have been based on two sources: the historical bread-of-life discourse and the Last Supper narrative of the institution of the Eucharist. Others have taken this step, and the result has been a theory of the origin of the bread-of-life discourse which daily gains more adherents among Catholics and non-Catholics.

This theory concentrates on both the historical setting of the discourse and the milieu in which the Gospel was written, admits the literary unity of the chapter, and looks to two sources for the teaching recorded in the bread-of-life discourse. It maintains that the historical bread-of-life discourse taught the necessity of faith in the person of Jesus and His doctrine. The eucharistic text, verses 52-59, is judged to be an addition inspired by the words of institution. Whether the author of the Fourth Gospel composed it himself or borrowed it from an oral tradition is an open question. Among those who maintain this opinion are M. E. Boismard, O.P., H. Schürmann and J. Jeremias. Also *La Sainte Bible de Jérusalem* (1956) maintains this theory.

In keeping with this general approach, it seems to this author that the question of the origin of the bread-of-life discourse should be answered as follows:

1. In the context of the Jewish Passover, Jesus taught that He was the Messiah who gives the bread of the Messianic age, who is Himself the Messianic bread of which the manna is a type, and who is the deliverer of all mankind in a redemption of which the Exodus is a type.

2. In accordance with the background of His audience, Jesus taught only implicitly the doctrine of the Eucharist and His calling to be the Suffering Servant who would die for all mankind.

3. In verses 52-59 John makes explicit what Christ implied in the bread-of-life discourse and revealed at the Last Supper.

4. The Jews and some of the disciples rejected Jesus' claim to be the unique mediator between God and man. John sees this rejection as an implicit denial of the eucharistic doctrine.

It will be noted that this explanation of the origin of the bread-of-life discourse integrates various elements of the interpretations we have already discussed. (1) By stressing the milieu in which the Gospel was written, this theory shows the validity of the traditional Catholic interpretation with its emphasis on the eucharistic teaching of the chapter. (2) By taking into account the historical context of the discourse, this theory shows the validity of the traditional Protestant interpretation with its emphasis on the aspect of faith. (3) By stressing the milieu in which the Gospel was written, this theory explains the eucharistic coloring of the whole chapter and the influence of the words of institution on certain verses. (4) This theory appeals to two sources, the historical bread-of-life discourse and the revelation of the Last Supper, which have been integrated by the author of the Fourth Gospel or by an oral tradition on which

he depended. (5) This theory appeals to the "two moments of understanding" advocated by Léon-Dufour to explain the option of the
hearers of the historical discourse, but it adds some nuances to that
explanation.

The Form of the Primitive Eucharist

HE EXTERNAL FORM of the eucharistic liturgies found in the churches of the East and West is the product of a long development. In the course of this evolution, one can detect four major stages which correspond in time to the Last Supper, the apostolic age, the postapostolic age up to the fourth century, and the advent of the great liturgies of the East and West. Although our main interest is centered on the practice in the first century, we will discuss briefly the changes which took place during the second, third, and fourth centuries, that is, up to the time when the great liturgies of the East and West began to take shape.

Basic to our analysis are the presuppositions that the words of institution are derived from the Last Supper and that the New Testament presents only one type of Eucharist. Both these presuppositions have been challenged by modern scholars. R. Bultmann and H. Lietzmann maintain that the Hellenistic Church was the unique source of the words of institution (cf. Chapter Two). However, in view of the research on the words of institution carried out during the past thirty years, this position has become increasingly unpopular. All the elements of the institutional accounts have been shown to be native to Jewish thought and hence point to a Palestinian origin completely independent of Greek mystery religions. The theory of two distinct types of Eucharist in the primitive Church, advocated especially by Lietzmann, has likewise proved unconvincing.

According to Lietzmann, two liturgical traditions are found in the New Testament. One indicates that the Eucharist is a joyful, eschatological meal (Acts 2:42-47); the other presents it as a sacramental meal (1 Cor. 11:23-25). Lietzmann thinks that the sacramental meal, originating in the Hellenistic milieu, finally prevailed and transformed the eschatological banquet into a mystery rite in which the commemoration of the sacrifice of Christ was joined with the eating of the Lord.

Not only does the Semitic background of the words of institution argue against Lietzmann's hypothesis of a *decisive* influence of Hellenistic mystery rites, but also there is no objective basis for asserting a rigid distinction between two types of Eucharist in the primitive Church. It is true that The Acts of the Apostles 2:42-47 present a picture of a joyful agape and that no mention is made in the text of a commemoration of the death of the Lord. Moreover, there is only a reference to "the breaking of the bread," without any mention of the blessing of the cup. So at first glance it would seem that the passage describes a meal at which wine was not drunk or at least was not important for the proceedings. Nevertheless, these observations are a weak foundation for postulating two types of Eucharist.

First, even granting for the sake of argument that the joyful expectation of the coming Kingdom may have relegated the memorial of Christ's death to the background of the primitive eucharistic celebrations in Jerusalem, there is no reason to think that it did not play an essential role. There is no contradiction between the two concepts, since the death of the Lord undergone for the salvation "of many" and ratified as efficacious by the glorious Resurrection and the sending of the Spirit was a source of joyful remembrance. The mystery of the cross was the basis of the hope to be fulfilled in the eschatological consummation. This joyful eschatological expectation is associated with the very words of institution in Mark 14:25; Matthew 26:29; Luke 22:15-18, 29-30; and Paul, who is supposed to have transformed the Palestinian eschatological feast into one that is predominantly a feast of the remembrance of Christ's death, expresses the harmony which exists between the concepts of "proclaiming the death of the Lord" and "until He comes." Thus in 1 Corinthians 11:26, St. Paul teaches that the Eucharist commemorates neither the past nor the future exclusively, but rather both: It is a proclamation of the death of the Lord until He comes.

Second, the contention of Lietzmann that The Acts of the Apostles 2:42-47 refers to wineless Eucharists, and thus distinguishes the Palestinian celebration from that of the Pauline tradition, is without solid basis. Such a conclusion can hardly be drawn in the name of history, as the argument from silence could scarcely be more fragile. One has but to consider the account of The Acts of the Apostles 20:7-11 which narrates how Paul met with the Christian community at Troas on the first day of the week "for the breaking of the bread." In this instance we are justified in concluding that the cup was used in accordance with Paul's teaching in 1 Corinthians 11:23-29. Now would the same phrase "breaking of the bread" in The Acts of the Apostles 2:42-47 exclude the cup at Jerusalem and include it at Troas? This theory would seem to be completely unacceptable.

Consequently, the New Testament testifies to a single Eucharist in bread and wine which bears the character of eschatological joy based on the remembrance of the redemptive death of the glorified Kyrios who is present in the eucharistic celebration *"in mysterio"* until His Second Coming. This Eucharist in turn finds its unique source in the words and gestures of Jesus at the Last Supper.

THE LAST SUPPER

The first celebration of the Eucharist was linked with a solemn festive meal which may have been the Paschal meal. Even if we take for granted that the Last Supper was a Paschal meal, there still remains the question of the exact procedure of the Paschal ritual of the first century. Since a great deal of uncertainty surrounds this whole problem, it need not concern us here. It suffices for us to know that the Last Supper was a solemn meal composed of three main parts: (1) the introductory prayer and distribution of bread, (2) the meal itself, (3) the solemn blessing over the last cup of wine.

As is indicated in Paul and Luke ("after the meal"), Jesus blessed the eucharistic bread at the beginning of the meal and the eucharistic wine at the end of the repast. Even if we did not have this remark of Paul and Luke, we could conclude that this procedure was followed from other considerations: (1) The introductory rite of the Jewish meal was a solemn religious gesture which included a prayer of praise and the breaking and distribution of bread by the leader. This was the only time that the leader distributed bread to all the participants. So important was this symbolic action which established table fellowship among the participants that anyone arriving afterwards was excluded from the meal. (2) 1 Corinthians 10:16 calls the eucharistic cup the "cup of blessing," a technical term for the cup associated with the end of the meal. (3) The fact that Jesus blessed the cup for all the participants indicates that it was the "cup of blessing." Only this cup was blessed by the leader for all. The other cups were most probably blessed by each of the participants for themselves.

From the foregoing evidence we conclude that the two consecrations were separated by the meal itself, whether it was a Paschal meal or an ordinary festive meal. Nevertheless, this separation in time did not affect the intimate relationship between the two consecrations. They are clearly related to one another and form a unified symbolic action which efficaciously represents the self-giving of the Servant of Yahweh. Bearing this in mind and the further consideration that the command to repeat the rite did not involve a meal properly so called, it is conceivable that the Eucharist could have been dissociated from a regular meal procedure from the beginning in the primitive Church. So the question arises: How did the Apostles celebrate the Eucharist after Christ's Ascension? Did they immediately separate it from a meal taken in the proper sense?

EUCHARISTIC PRACTICE IN APOSTOLIC TIMES

There is only one text which discusses at length the actual celebration of the Eucharist in the primitive Church. 1 Corinthians 11:17-34 testifies that the Eucharist was celebrated in conjunction with a fraternal meal at Corinth (cf. Chapter Three). This fact, however, does not prove that the Eucharist was always and everywhere linked to a meal in the apostolic period. Moreover, the evidence from The Acts of the Apostles concerning the mode of celebrating the Eucharist at Jerusalem and Troas does not give us much information on the point at issue (Acts 2:42, 46; 20:7-11).

Several times in The Acts of the Apostles reference is made to "the breaking of the bread." In Jewish circles this term was used to designate an action which included the prayer of praise of Yahweh and the breaking of bread at the beginning of the meal. It was related to the meal which followed. Christians borrowed the term and used it as a technical expression for the Eucharist. Thus in The Acts of the Apostles 2:42 the "breaking of the bread" refers to a completely self-contained act which is set in a liturgical context: It is linked with (1) the teaching of the Apostles, (2) *koinōnia* (fellowship of Christians united in worship), (3) prayer. The term is a Christian mode of expression alien to Jewish and classical literature. It refers to the holy bread of the Lord's Supper.

The second reference to "the breaking of bread" occurs in The Acts of the Apostles 2:46: "And continuing daily with one accord in the temple, and breaking bread in their houses, they took their food with gladness and simplicity of heart, praising God and being in favor with all the people." Again, this reference does not tell us much about the relationship of the Eucharist to a communal meal. It is not stated that the "breaking of bread" took place daily or that it was linked to a communal meal.

A final reference to "breaking bread" in a liturgical context is found in The Acts of the Apostles 20:7-11. Paul had gone to Troas, a city in Asia Minor, to visit the Christian community. In the course of his stay of seven days, it is related that he attended a gathering which was held "on the first day of the week" (this could have been Saturday night or Sunday evening since the Jewish sabbath ended at sundown). The main purpose of the meeting was "to break bread." This was accomplished under the direction of Paul in an upper chamber after he had delivered a long exhortation. The fact that there were "many lamps" in the room seems to indicate a solemn liturgical setting.

This description of a eucharistic celebration indicates that the usual time for the "breaking of the bread" was the first day of the week, the day on which Christ rose from the dead. But we learn nothing of the actual relationship of the Eucharist to an agape. Since the main meal of the day was taken in the evening, we may conjecture that a meal accompanied the Eucharist at Troas, but that is all. However, it would seem that the practice observed at Corinth was common to the whole Church at this early date. We learn from Luke 24:42 that the common meal provided the occasion for the gathering of the Apostles after the Resurrection of Christ. After Pentecost such meals would be the natural time for the celebration of the Lord's Supper.

On the assumption that the Eucharist was ordinarily, if not always, linked to a fraternal meal in the primitive Church, the problem arises concerning the way in which the Eucharist was joined to the meal. Did the primitive Church follow the same pattern as the celebration which took place at the Last Supper? It has been conjectured that the phrase "after the meal" found in 1 Corinthians 11:25 indicates that the meal of the community was placed between the two consecrations after the example of the Last Supper. Paul is supposed to have inserted this phrase to manifest his wish to maintain the meal, though rightly ordered and enclosed by the consecrations of the bread and wine. However, this interpretation overlooks several important facts. First, the beginning of the meal, at least at Corinth, was unregulated, as is clear from verses 21 and 33. Hence, it would seem natural that the consecration of the bread and wine would take place at the end of the meal when all were present. Moreover, the formula of the words of institution handed on by Paul is a liturgical unit which gives every indication of having been recited in one continuous action over the bread and wine. It may be that the phrase "after the meal" is not intended merely as an historical note which is allowed to survive in the liturgical formula. There may be other considerations of a liturgical character which account for its presence (cf. Chapter Seven for a possible explanation). Nevertheless, the interpretation mentioned above cannot be reconciled with the context of 1 Corinthians 11:17-34.

Actually, all the New Testament evidence points to the conclusion that early in Apostolic times, perhaps before the year forty (the time of the formation of the Antioch-Palestinian formula of institution), the double consecration was joined together and placed at the end of the agape. The evidence for this conclusion may be summarized as follows:

I. *The double consecration was joined together very early.*

1. The symmetrical style of all the accounts of the institution indicates that they formed literary units which were recited as such at one point in the liturgical proceedings.

2. The formulations found in Mark and Matthew give no indication that a meal separated the two consecrations even at the Last Supper. The picture presented is that of one continuous action over the bread and wine.

II. *The eucharistic celebration was placed at the end of the agape.*

1. At Corinth, according to the testimony of 1 Corinthians 11:17-34, it would appear that the Eucharist was celebrated at the end of the agape since the meal did not begin in common (vv. 21, 33).

2. It was natural that the eucharistic celebration should take place at the most solemn part of the festive meal, that is, the end of the repast when the solemn prayer was spoken over the cup of wine. The fact that Paul designates the eucharistic cup as "the cup of blessing" (1 Cor. 10:16), the cup over which the grace-after-meals was recited, is an indication that the consecration of the wine took place at this time. Since this consecration was linked to that of the bread, the whole eucharistic action must have taken place at the end of the meal.

3. The *symposion* at the end of the festive meal occasioned hymns and songs. Hence, it was a good point of departure for the eucharistic celebration which involved the singing of pious hymns, as the New Testament shows (Eph. 5:19; Col. 3:16).

4. Remnants of the Jewish grace-after-meals are found to survive in the eucharistic prayers of all early liturgies. Hence, we have another link between the Eucharist and the conclusion of a festive meal.

From the foregoing observations, we conclude that early in the primitive Church, probably before the year forty, the double consecration was placed at the end of a fraternal meal. The whole procedure was called "the Lord's Supper" at Corinth (1 Cor. 11:20). Nevertheless, though bound to a meal, the Eucharist retains relative independence. It is the only part of the meal which is repeated at the invitation of Christ as a memorial of His saving activity.

With this development, the Eucharist is on its way to a completely independent existence, which it will eventually attain in the second century. In the meantime, the Jewish grace-after-meals will be adapted in various ways to express a remembrance of the redemptive work wrought through Christ. The enlargement of this solemn prayer was often associated with the composition of a number of liturgical hymns commemorating the redeemer and His work. Precipitates of these hymns can be found in various New Testament writings (John 1:1-18; Col. 1:15-20; Phil. 2:5-11; 1 Tim. 3:16; and so on).

EUCHARISTIC PRACTICE IN THE POST-APOSTOLIC AGE TO THE FOURTH CENTURY

We do not know exactly when the Eucharist began to be celebrated apart from an agape. It certainly did not occur everywhere at the same time. We know, for example, that in Egypt in the fifth century the Eucharist was celebrated by the Christian communities on Saturday after a meal. Moreover, in the domestic celebrations which continued alongside the larger community celebrations, the meal was retained much longer because the practical problem of serving a meal to a considerable number of participants did not exist.

It has been argued that the first clue to the separation of the agape from the Eucharist is found in a letter which Pliny the Younger, Proconsul of Bithynia (A.D. 111-113), addressed to the Emperor Trajan. In this letter Pliny tells how he apprehended some Christians and interrogated them concerning their way of life. In the course of the discussion, they told him about their assemblies. It was their practice to gather before dawn on a fixed day to sing a hymn to Christ their God and to bind themselves by oath to do no wrong. Later on the same day they met together again to participate in a communal meal. After hearing the testimony, Pliny forbade the continuation of the meal.

According to some authors the morning meeting was a eucharistic celebration. Thus, they interpret the reference to the singing of a hymn to Christ as an allusion to the Eucharist. The oath to do no wrong would refer to a public confession of sins as a preparation for the participation in the Lord's Supper. Other authors, however, believe that the first gathering did not involve a eucharistic banquet but rather a renewal of the baptismal oath. They contend that Pliny would not have forbidden a simple fraternal meal in the evening, and so they maintain that the later gathering included a cultic action, a eucharistic celebration. If this interpretation is correct, the Eucharist was still bound to a meal at Bithynia at this time.

What we do know with certainty is that the separation of the Eucharist from the agape had taken place in some areas of the Church by the middle of the second century. Justin Martyr, in his *First Apology,* Chapters 65-67, describes a eucharistic celebration which takes place on Sunday morning in conjunction with a liturgical service modeled on the Jewish synagogue ritual. It had the following form:

1. Lessons were read from the memoirs (Epistles and Gospels) of the Apostles.
2. A sermon, based on the lesson, was given by the priest.
3. Prayers of intercession were made in common.
4. The kiss of peace was given.
5. The eucharistic prayer was recited. This was a long prayer of praise and thanksgiving with no set form, but which always included a commemoration of the redemptive work of Christ and the words of institution of the Eucharist. The celebrant proclaimed this prayer and the people answered *Amen* as an affirmation of their part in the liturgical worship.
6. Communion followed in which the celebrant, deacons, and people received the eucharistic bread and wine.
7. A collection of money was taken up to be given by the priest to the poor.

This form of the liturgy was probably used in the greater part of the Western Church for congregational assemblies in the middle of the second century, especially in Rome and among its dependent churches. The elements of this liturgy are recognizable in all later forms of the eucharistic liturgy.

We can only conjecture as to the cause of the separation of the agape from the Eucharist. In the final analysis it seems that the growth of the Christian community was a major factor. The meal became impractical when the community had expanded. It is also possible that abuses associated with the agape, such as those which Paul encountered at Corinth, may have contributed to the separation.

Several important consequences followed the removal of the agape from the Eucharist. The arrangement of the place set aside for the Lord's Supper underwent a change. One table alone remained for the celebrant, and the room was enlarged to accommodate the growing number of participants. A change also took place in the time of the celebration of the Eucharist. The principal meal was ordinarily held in the evening; and as long as the Eucharist was linked to an agape it was celebrated on Saturday night or Sunday evening, the day of Christ's Resurrection. However, when the separation of the agape was effected, it could be transferred to Sunday morning at sunrise, the actual time of the Resurrection according to the traditional belief. This transfer was made during the first half of the second century in many areas.

The omission of the agape caused the Eucharist to lose, to some extent, the form of a meal. The action of the celebrant was stressed over that of the other participants. The amplified eucharistic prayer dominated the whole procedure. However, the Eucharist did retain the character of a symbolic festive meal and was recognized as such. Justin, for example, speaks of the consecrated bread and wine as food (*First Apology,* Chapter 66), and the eucharistic prayer which he describes in the *Dialogue with Trypho,* Chapter 41, is patterned on the Jewish grace-after-meals (cf. Chapter Six).

At the beginning of the third century, the *Apostolic Tradition* of Hippolytus (circa A.D. 215) presents us with the first complete text of a eucharistic liturgy. It fits the general description found in Justin's *First Apology,* where the agape was replaced by the liturgy of the word. The eucharistic prayer, which Hippolytus suggests, remains within the general framework of the Jewish grace-after-meals and includes the remembrance of the redemptive work of Christ and the words of institution (cf. Chapter Six).

During the rest of the third century and well into the fourth century, the general picture remains the same. The available evidence shows that the Eucharist, even after the separation from the agape, retained the character of a symbolic festive meal. The consecrated elements are considered food, and the eucharistic prayer is modeled on the Jewish grace-after-meals.

THE SHAPE OF THE EUCHARIST IN THE GREAT LITURGIES

In the fourth century, as a result of the Edict of Milan, the Church began to flourish. The liturgies of the East and West grew in richness. Complicated formularies and ceremonies, mirroring the geniuses of the various cultures, were added. All this tended to obscure the basic form of the primitive Eucharist. Christians would have to be reminded constantly of the purpose of the gatherings: to participate in the Lord's Supper both by uniting themselves to the offering of the eucharistic Christ and by communicating in the consecrated food. This was a totally new phenomenon, unknown in the previous centuries. Until the fourth century communion was normally received by all in attendance. Afterwards—it is difficult to judge exactly when—a falling off in frequent communion took place in some areas of the Church. By the end of the fourth century, John Chrysostom, in the East, found it necessary to complain: "In vain we stand before the altar; there is no one to partake" (*Homily on the Epistle to the Ephesians* 3:4). In the West, Ambrose mentions the problem of frequent communion in a sermon in which he exhorts the newly baptized to receive frequently and not to follow the custom among the Greeks of receiving once a year (*De Sacramentis* 5:25). It has been suggested by some authors that Ambrose does not envision this pastoral problem as existing in the Church of Milan and is simply encouraging the new converts to take advantage of the privilege of frequent reception of the bread of life. But it is hardly likely that he would have introduced the question of frequent communion if the contrary practice was not widespread.

This change in practice may have been caused by several factors. The recognition of Christianity as the religion of the state occasioned the conversion of numerous pagans. This new body of Christians, many of whom entered the Church for reasons of expediency rather than for purely religious motives, undoubtedly exerted great influence on the traditional attitude of Christians toward the Eucharist. A parallel case can be found in the practice of delaying baptism, which became fairly widespread among Christians during the first half of the fourth century. All the evidence at hand indicates that this usage originated with pagan converts at the beginning of the fourth century.

Another reason for the neglect of frequent communion can be found in the changing theological outlook concerning the Eucharist which resulted from the Arian dispute over the essential divinity of the Son. The stress on Christ's divinity so influenced the general attitude of Christians toward the Eucharist that the sacrament of the real presence of the *Son of God* was placed beyond the reach of ordinary, sinful men. John Chrysostom calls the Eucharist "a table of holy fear," "the frightful mysteries," "the mysteries which demand reverence and trembling." The consecrated wine is called "the cup of holy awe," "the awe-inspiring blood." The Eucharist is the "awe-inspiring and terrible sacrifice," "a fearful and holy sacrifice."

It is true that John Chrysostom stresses that the Eucharist is a banquet: "Believe that there takes place now the same banquet as that in which Christ sat at table, and that this banquet is in no way different from that" (*Homily on the Betrayal of Judas* 2:6); and he does speak often of the eucharistic "table." Nevertheless, the concept of easy access associated with a banquet is not present. The stress is on the "aweful mysteries" and the demand for careful preparation.

In considering the general shape that the Eucharist takes in the great liturgies, we can view the Roman Mass as typical. The Canon of the Mass contains many words or expressions which speak of "sacrifice" and "offering sacrifice." Only once do we find a reference to the setting forth of a repast. It is the *"sumpserimus"* of the *Supplices* prayer which looks ahead to the subsequent part of the eucharistic celebration: Communion. The idea of a sacrifice being offered runs through the whole of the Canon, beginning with the *Te Igitur*. In the Preface it is said: "It is truly meet and just, right and salutary that we should at all times and in all places give thanks unto Thee. . . ." Then the Canon begins: "We therefore. . . ." In view of the remarks made in the Preface, this introduction indicates that we are going to do something. What are we going to do? The answer is given: "We therefore humbly pray . . . that Thou wouldst vouchsafe to receive and bless these gifts, these offerings, these holy and unblemished sacrifices." We ask the Father to accept the sacrifice from our hands since it is our task to give thanks and praise God.

The Canon is a typical sacrificial prayer in which the Church indicates her desire to offer sacrifice. The repast begins, in the traditional shape of the great liturgies, after the sacrificial action is complete. The Canon is a preparation for the repast, but it has an independent value and character of its own. It is the offering of the sacrifice of the new covenant.

What the great liturgies have done is to emphasize the distinction between the two essential elements of the Eucharist: (1) the offering of the covenant sacrifice and (2) the communion in the sacrificial food. These essential elements, although recognized in the earlier forms of the Eucharist were not so clearly distinguished, nor need they have been for a people who understood the full implications of a *covenant meal*.

Chapter
Six

The Structure and Content of
the Primitive Eucharistic Prayer

IN CHAPTER FIVE we learned that the Eucharist was linked to a fraternal meal in the apostolic age. Moreover, all the evidence points to the conclusion that very early in the primitive Church both consecrations were placed together at the end of the meal. This arrangement was to be expected for it placed the Eucharist at the most solemn part of the banquet, the moment when the prayer of blessing was pronounced over the cup of wine by the leader. Bearing this in mind and the further observation that the early Christians did not completely reject their Jewish heritage in religious matters, it would not be surprising if the prayers recited in connection with the consecration of the bread and wine were modeled on the Jewish grace-after-meals. It was only natural for Christians to draw on the traditional form of prayer they knew and to simply refashion it so that it conformed to the new revelation of salvation through Jesus Christ.

What then was the form of the Jewish grace-after-meals and what is the evidence that Christians modeled their eucharistic prayers on it? And what is more important: How did the content of the eucharistic prayer differ from the Jewish table prayer?

We can begin to answer these questions with an analysis of the fundamental structure of *blessings* found in the Old Testament and in Jewish liturgical prayers. In these blessings there is an initial doxology (a prayer of praise addressed to Yahweh), which is followed by a remembrance of the particularly mighty works of Yahweh which motivate the prayer. Thus, in Genesis 24:27, the servant of Abraham prays: "Blessed be the Lord, the God of my master Abraham [doxology] who has not forsaken His steadfast love and His faithfulness towards my master [proclamation of Yahweh's faithfulness]."

In the more formal liturgical prayers, a final doxology is added which returns to the initial one. An example of this type is found in the Kiddush, the Jewish prayer of sanctification for the Sabbath. Often prayers of intercession are also included, as in the case of the Jewish grace-after-meals.

Christ followed this manner of praying during the course of His public life, as is indicated in John 11:41 and Matthew 11:25, and He did so at the Last Supper when He "gave thanks" over the bread and wine. The Greek word *eucharistein,* used to express Christ's action at the time of the institution of the Eucharist, should be rendered as a translation of *bārak,* which means "to bless or praise" rather than "to give thanks." Indeed, both Mark and Matthew use *eulogein* (to bless, praise) when describing Jesus' prayer over the eucharistic bread. Hence, at the Last Supper, Jesus set the words of institution in the context of a solemn proclamation in joyous praise of the mighty deeds of His Father in accomplishing the salvation of mankind through the Son.

The primitive Church observed the same form in her liturgical prayer, as is shown by the many doxologies and hymns found in the New Testament. Concerning the *direct* dependence of the eucharistic prayers of the primitive Church on the Jewish grace-after-meals, the *textual* evidence is not sufficient to give us certainty in the matter. However, as soon as undisputed eucharistic prayers begin to appear in patristic literature, they show so close a similarity to the Jewish grace-after-meals that a relationship of dependence seems certain. One can then argue that if this is true for the second and third century, it must have been true for the first century. In other words, the necessary and sufficient reason for the close parallel between the Jewish grace-after-meals and the second- and third-century eucharistic prayers is the heritage derived from the first century when the Eucharist was joined to a fraternal banquet and celebrated at the point where the grace-after-meals was recited in the ordinary Jewish communal meal.

As proof of the dependence of the second- and third-century eucharistic prayers on the Jewish grace-after-meals, we need but compare the latter with the formula recorded by Justin Martyr in his *Dialogue with Trypho,* Chapter 41 (circa A.D. 155), and that of Hippolytus contained in his *Apostolic Tradition* 4 (circa A.D. 215).

JEWISH TABLE PRAYER	DIALOGUE WITH TRYPHO 41	APOSTOLIC TRADITION 4
Doxology.	*Doxology.*	*Doxology.*
Remembrance of gifts of nourishment, promised land,	*Remembrance* of gifts of creation,	*Remembrance* of gifts of Christ, creator of the world,
redemption from Egypt, knowledge of Law,	redemption from evil through Christ,	redemption from suffering, death, devils,
covenant,	covenant sacrifice of New Law,	covenant and establishment of a holy people,
life,	Resurrection of Christ,	manifestation of Resurrection,
daily food.	institution of Eucharist (cf. Justin's *1 Apology* 66 for words of institution).	institution of Eucharist, death and Resurrection of Christ.
Intercession for Israel, Jerusalem (Temple restoration in later times), Messiah, participants of banquet.	*Omitted.*	*Intercession* for coming of Spirit made over the oblation (interpolation), reception of Spirit by participants.
Final Doxology.	*Omitted.*	*Final Doxology.*

When we attempt a similar comparison with first-century eucharistic prayers, the obvious difficulty arises that there is no liturgical text which is of certainty a eucharistic prayer related to the actual celebration of the Eucharist. Nevertheless, there is good reason for maintaining that Colossians 1:12-20 and Chapters 59-61 of the *First Epistle* of Pope Clement are derivatives of a eucharistic prayer. And finally, Chapters 9-10 of the *Didache* most probably contain a liturgical prayer linked to the actual celebration of the Lord's Supper. All three texts bear a striking resemblance to the Jewish grace-after-meals.

COLOSSIANS 1:12-20 (9-11)	1 CLEMENT 59-61	DIDACHE 9-10
Doxology (12).	Doxology (59:2, reconstructed).	Doxology (9:1, 3; 10: 2, 4).
Remembrance of gifts of creation by Christ (15-20),	Remembrance of gifts of creation (59:2-3),	Remembrance of gifts of creation and nourishment (10:3).
election of inheritance of kingdom (12-13),	election through Christ (59:2),	Omitted.
liberation from the powers of darkness	liberation from darkness to light,	
and remission of sins (13-14),	from ignorance to knowledge (59:2),	Knowledge (9:3; 10: 2) and faith (10:2).
Kingdom of Christ (13) and Church (18a),	new people of God (59:4),	Omitted.
Resurrection (18a) and inheritance of the saints in light,	life (59:3) and sanctification (59:3).	immortality (10:2) and eternal life (10: 3),
allusion to eucharistic bread (18a) and eucharistic blood (20).	Omitted.	"spiritual food and drink" (10:3).
Intercession for knowledge and grace (9-11).	Intercession for needy (59:4), Church (59:4), pardon for sins (60:1-2), peace (60:4), rulers (61:1-2).	Intercession for Church (9:4; 10:5), parousia (10:6).
Omitted.	Final Doxology (61:3).	Final Doxology (9:2, 3; 10:2, 4, 6).

This outline indicates a certain influence of the Jewish form of prayer on the liturgical texts of the primitive Christian Church. It also furnishes probable evidence of an intimate relationship between the Jewish table prayer and the primitive eucharistic prayer.

Thus far we have dealt with the outward form of the early eucharistic prayer and its relationship to the Jewish grace-after-meals. We concluded that the liturgical prayers of Justin and Hippolytus are certainly dependent, regarding outward form, on the Jewish table prayer. To some extent, the content of both prayers is also similar, but there are certain peculiarities which clearly distinguish the Christian version. First, in the Christian blessing there is an explicit or implicit reference to the command of Christ to celebrate the Eucharist in remembrance of Him. Second, the chief element of the remembrance, though not the exclusive subject, is the redemptive work of Christ. Third, the words of institution used by Christ at the Last Supper are recited over the bread and wine. These three elements are found in the most ancient types of eucharistic prayer, with the exception of the liturgy of Addai and Mari and the so-called Persian Anaphora, an ancient Mesopotamian liturgical text, which do not contain the words of institution. Whether these anaphoras originally gave the account of the institution is disputed. In any case, the liturgy of Addai and Mari alludes to the institution of the Eucharist in the phrase "We . . . have received from tradition the example which is from Thee." The Persian Anaphora also refers to the institution of the Eucharist and the command of Christ to do as He had done.

The basic similarity between the content of the Jewish table prayer and the earliest eucharist prayers, which harken back to first-century usage, is the orientation toward the worship of God. This primary concern is brought out by the initial and final doxologies. Although the memorial aspect of both prayers is centered on the saving work of God in history, there is a difference in the content of the remembrance: the eucharistic prayers recalling the completion of salvation history in Christ. The eucharistic prayers bear witness that the Lord's Supper has a religious value because of the redemptive work of Christ. Without this memorial aspect, the liturgical action would not be Christian; it would not pertain to the new covenant.

In conclusion, we may say that the fundamental structure and content of the most ancient eucharistic prayers, which indicate first-century usage, reveal that the liturgical action of the Christian community is first and foremost an act of adoration of God, just as is the Jewish counterpart. But the doxology is followed by a remembrance of the redemptive work of Christ, which proclaims that this act of adoration is acceptable because it is accomplished through the one mediator Jesus Christ who is sacramentally present to His people in order to draw them, by means of the visible ritual, into His acceptable sacrificial offering. It is this aspect of the eucharistic prayer which distinguishes it from the liturgical prayer of the Jewish tradition and which gives it an efficacy unthinkable in the old dispensation.

The Eucharistic Cup in the Primitive Liturgy

THE WORDS OF INTERPRETATION spoken over the cup at the Last Supper express dramatically and explicitly the meaning of the Eucharist as re-presentation of the redemptive death of Christ which seals the covenant. Moreover, the cup itself, independently of the significance given to it at the Last Supper, was already employed by Christ as a symbol of His sufferings (Mark 10:38; 14:36; John 18:11).

But if the cup objectively holds the central place in the eucharistic celebration, the phrase "the blessing of the cup" was not used to designate the Eucharist in the primitive Church. At Corinth a common name for the Eucharist was "the Lord's Supper" (1 Cor. 11:20), but this term embraced both the agape and the Eucharist taken together. To designate the Eucharist itself the phrase "the breaking of the bread" (Acts 2:42, 46; 20:7-11) was used. Thus surprisingly enough when one of the essential parts of the eucharistic celebration is selected to represent the whole action, that part is chosen which is less prominent, less strongly accentuated in the essential rite instituted by Christ.

So unexpected is the designation of the Eucharist as "the breaking of the bread" that some exegetes have concluded that it implies wineless Eucharists. We have already discussed this theory and have found it wanting. The fact that the cup is not mentioned is entirely too fragile a basis for concluding that it was omitted from the celebration. It is true that in the third century there is evidence of a fairly widespread rejection of the cup among heterodox Christians, but this was inspired by principles of asceticism associated with a Gnostic mentality. The Church Fathers unhesitatingly condemned it as foreign to the ancient tradition of the Church. There is, then, only the argument of silence for the assertion that the cup was omitted in orthodox usage among the primitive Christians. It has never been shown that the primitive Church accepted wineless Eucharists as legitimate. Hence, the presumption is against the interpretation of "the breaking of the bread" as implying wineless Eucharists.

Moreover, as was observed in Chapter Five, The Acts of the Apostles 20:7-11 deals with Paul's celebration of the Eucharist at Troas and describes it as "the breaking of the bread." In this instance we are justified in concluding that the cup was used in accordance with Paul's teaching in 1 Corinthians 11:23-29. Hence, there is no basis for saying that the same phrase in The Acts of the Apostles 2:42, 46 indicates wineless Eucharists were conducted at Jerusalem.

If the phrase "the breaking of the bread" was not used to designate wineless eucharistic banquets, we are still left with the problem: Why was the Eucharist so designated? J. Jeremias' suggestion that the term is a cryptogram is quite possible. But it still leaves unanswered the more fundamental question: Why was this phrase used and not, for example, "the blessing of the cup"? This latter question has never been satisfactorily answered. Since the eucharistic cup objectively is more important in the liturgical action, it would seem only natural that preference would be extended to the phrase "the blessing of the cup."

Although we make no pretences at being able to solve this problem with any degree of certainty, there are some reasons which can explain the use of the phrase "the breaking of the bread." First, the ordinary gesture of breaking the bread in accordance with Jewish table customs took on a new and unparalleled significance because of the words of interpretation spoken by Christ at the Last Supper. Recognizing that the blessing of the bread is as important as the blessing of the wine, the primitive Church would have an objective basis for referring to the whole rite as the "breaking of the bread." The actual choice of the phrase may have been influenced by the fact that in its commonly accepted meaning, it embraced the whole rite which introduced the Jewish meal [eulogia (blessing), breaking of bread, distribution]. Thus, the term did stand for the whole ritual action over the bread. Being the designation for the introductory rite of the eucharistic celebration, it could fittingly serve as a name for the whole rite which included the blessing and distribution of the cup. The phrase "the blessing of the cup," which implicitly included the distribution, could just as easily have been used. However, it seems quite natural that of the two essential actions, objectively equal in importance, that one which comes first would be selected to stand as *pars pro toto*. Moreover, in a meal setting, the act of eating is more accentuated than the act of drinking. Thus, Paul speaks of eating the Lord's Supper (1 Cor. 11:20), and the Synoptics refer to the eating of the Last Supper, though in both cases wine was included. The form of a meal which the Eucharist takes may, accordingly, have influenced the use of the term "breaking of the bread." Finally, the manna of the desert, looked on as a type of the Eucharist, probably exerted some influence on the choice of the term (John 6; 1 Cor. 10:3).

Nevertheless, although the phrase "breaking of the bread" was the characteristic name given to the primitive eucharistic celebrations, it does not imply that the cup, in actual practice, was placed in the background. Just the opposite seems to have been true. In the following pages we will examine texts which show that the cup was emphasized more than the bread. In each case practical motives which could have led to this emphasis will be considered.

1 Corinthians 11:25; Luke 22:20: "after the meal"

The Pauline and Lukan tradition mentions that at the Last Supper Jesus blessed the eucharistic cup "after the meal." No reference is made to the exact time when the blessing of the bread took place. This fact alone draws attention to the cup. But why is the cup mentioned? Is it merely an historical note which survives in the liturgical formula? It would seem that more significance should be attached to this phrase, especially since it is characteristic of the accounts of institution to drop unnecessary historical details, to retain only that which is necessary for the essential liturgical action.

In Chapter Five we learned that very early in the apostolic age the double consecration was joined together and placed at the end of an agape, as 1 Corinthian 11:17-34 testifies. Thus, the phrase "after the meal" does not assure the insertion of the agape between the two consecrations. Nevertheless, the retention of the phrase seems to have been motivated by liturgical interest: to make certain of the identification of the eucharistic cup with the cup over which the solemn grace-after-meals was recited at the conclusion of a festive meal.

There are three probable reasons for this insistence. First, it would guarantee that the whole eucharistic celebration, which took place as one continuous action, would be situated after the agape when all were assembled and not in the midst of the disorder so frequently associated with the beginning of the agape, as is stated in 1 Corinthians 11:33. Second, it would assure the link between the Eucharist and the solemn grace-after-meals. This prayer of praise which Jewish custom prescribed before the drinking of the "cup of blessing" was most appropriate to introduce the memorial of the Last Supper. Third, it emphasized the solemn, festive character of the Eucharist. The cup which was drunk at the end of the festive meal introduced the festive drinking (*mishtītā; symposion*) which distinguished the common meal from the feast. By situating the eucharistic cup at that part of the festive meal where the festive drinking usually began, the solemn, festive character of the Eucharist was emphasized.

Mark 14:23b: "and they all drank of it"

Here is another instance where an historical detail is introduced into the liturgical formula and by its presence lays stress on the cup. As in the case of the phrase "after the meal," it would seem to imply more than an interest in the historical details of the Last Supper. Mark stresses what is clearly understood, although not mentioned explicitly, in all the other accounts of institution.

Various explanations have been given for the presence of this bit of information which, at first glance, seems altogether superfluous. One opinion maintains that the phrase is introduced to instruct the faithful that they should use one cup in accordance with the unusual practice which Christ employed at the Last Supper. This theory presupposes that each one had his own cup at the Paschal meal or at an ordinary festive meal and that Jesus inaugurated a

new custom by insisting that the Apostles drink from one cup. However, evidence for this opinion is lacking. We simply do not know
enough about this custom in the first century; and in any case,
it is extremely doubtful that the question of individual cup versus
common cup would have had such an important place in the liturgical practice of the primitive Church. Finally, in the Markan account the emphasis is placed on the blood. The word "cup" does
not appear in the actual words of institution. The phrase in question, therefore, presumably refers to the wine designated as the
blood of Christ: "and they all drank of it" (the blood of the covenant).

Another interpretation maintains that the phrase with *pantes*
(all) placed at the end of the sentence emphasizes that Jesus ab-
stained from drinking. This theory is hardly likely. Although Jesus
did abstain from drinking, what seems to be stressed is simply that
all the Apostles drank of the sacramental blood of Christ.

This phrase seems to betray a polemic interest. It may well be
an appeal to the authority of the Apostles for the legality and fruit-
fulness of drinking the blood of Christ. It is quite conceivable that
this phrase is directed against certain factions in the primitive
Jewish-Christian community which rejected the cup through a
deep-rooted fear of blood. It is possible that in the primitive Church
of the Palestinian milieu, among those who held fast to the Mosaic
Law (Acts 21:20) and placed the blood ban on Gentile converts
(Acts 15:29), a radical Pharisaic wing (Acts 15:5) went so far as to
promote a definite antipathy for the cup and made of the blood of
Christ a stumbling block.

1 Corinthians 11:25b: "as often as you drink"

Another remark which causes the cup to stand out more prominently than the bread is found in the Pauline account of the institution of the Eucharist. The phrase "as often as you drink" does
not refer to the possibility of wineless Eucharists, as is clear from
verse 26 where the same words "as often as" recur with reference
to the bread and the cup. Much less is this phrase concerned with
a non-eucharistic cup, as a glance at 1 Corinthians 11:21 and Ephesians 5:18 will show. What then is its significance?

It has been conjectured that it betrays anxiety on the part of Paul to forestall any impropriety in the eucharistic service. The Corinthians should realize that this cup, as the unique cup, should be blessed and shared in remembrance of the Lord. All other drinking of wine should be excluded from the Lord's Supper except that connected with the Eucharist so as to guard against the shameful conduct alluded to in 1 Corinthians 11:21. Although the Corinthians would not always drink wine and hold the Eucharist at a communal meal, nevertheless if the meal was celebrated in a festive way with the Eucharist, then the eucharistic cup, as the unique cup, would be emptied in remembrance of the Lord. What St. Paul is saying may be paraphrased in this way: "do this" equals drink this unique cup, "the cup of blessing," in remembrance of the Kyrios; "as often as you drink" equals as often as you celebrate the Eucharist in the course of a festive meal where wine is ordinarily drunk. Or to put it another way: "You will, as is customary, drink wine in the course of a festive meal. That drinking will, however, be limited in the case where the Eucharist is joined to the feast, to the " 'cup of blessing' " which is drunk in remembrance of the Lord"

Although this interpretation is attractive, it remains only probable. The phrase in question may simply mean "everytime you drink" and imply that wine is as necessary as bread for the Eucharist. Support for this explanation can be found in verse 26 where the words "as often as" recur. Thus, Paul may be emphasizing the necessity of wine for the Eucharist, lest his rebuke about excessive drinking at the agape be interpreted to exclude all wine drinking from the liturgical celebration.

Conclusion

We have studied three texts which indicate the special preoccupation of the primitive Church with the eucharistic cup. The fact seems beyond dispute, but we can only conjecture the reasons for the interest. It would seem that a desire to preserve right order, to maintain intact the rite handed down by the Lord, and to emphasize the solemnity of the Lord's Supper resulted in the accentuation of the eucharistic cup.

Selected Bibliography

The following periodical and book list represents references which the author found particularly helpful for his own study. References to the works of authors whose names occur in the text of this book will be found by consulting the bibliography which is arranged according to chapter and theme.

CHAPTER ONE

I. *The Prophecy of Malachi*
Pautrel, R., "Malachie," *Dictionnaire de la Bible, Supplément* V (1957), cols 743-45.

II. *The Sacrifice of Melchizedek*
Fitzmyer, J. A., " 'Now This Melchizedek . . .' (Heb 7, 1)," *Catholic Biblical Quarterly*, XXV (1963), pp. 305-21.

III. *Messianic Banquet and Heavenly Manna*
Daniélou, J., "Les repas de la Bible et leur signification," *Maison Dieu*, XVIII (1948), pp. 7-33.
———, *The Bible and the Liturgy* (Notre Dame, Ind.: University of Notre Dame Press, 1956), pp. 142-61.
Feuillet, A., "Les thèmes bibliques majeurs du discours sur le pain de vie," *Nouvelle Revue Théologique*, LXXXII (1960), pp. 803-22, 918-1062.

IV. *Sacrificial Blood*
Dewar, L., "The Biblical Use of the Term Blood," *Journal of Theological Studies*, IV (1953), pp. 204-8.
Steinmueller, J., "Sacrificial Blood in the Bible," *Biblica*, XL (1959), pp. 556-67.

CHAPTER TWO

I. *Representative Opinions Concerning the Origin and Meaning of the Words of Institution*

Allo, E. B., *Saint Paul, Première épître aux Corinthiens* (Paris: J. Gabalda, 1934), pp. 294-316.

Bultmann, R., *Theology of the New Testament* I (London: SCM Press Ltd, 1952), pp. 144-52.

Coppens, J., "Eucharistie," *Dictionnaire de la Bible Supplément* II (1934), cols 1146-1215.

———, "Miscellanées bibliques XXIV," *Ephemerides Theologicae Lovanienses,* XXXIII (1957), pp. 483-510.

Cullmann, O., *Early Christian Worship* (Naperville, Ill.: Alec R. Allenson, Inc., 1953), pp. 14-19.

———, "The Meaning of the Lord's Supper in Primitive Christianity," *Essays on the Lord's Supper,* Ecumenical Studies in Worship I (London: Lutterworth Press, 1958).

Dix, G., *The Shape of the Liturgy* (Westminster: Dacre Press, 1945), pp. 48-102.

Higgins, A. J. B., *The Lord's Supper in the New Testament* (Chicago: Henry Regnery Co., 1952), pp. 56-63 and passim.

Jeremias, J., *Eucharistic Words of Jesus* (Oxford: Basil Blackwell, 1955), pp. 144-46, 165 and passim.

Kuhn, K. G., "The Lord's Supper and the Communal Meal at Qumran," *The Scrolls and the New Testament,* ed. K. Stendahl (New York: Harper, 1957), pp. 65-93.

Leenhardt, F. J., *Le Sacrament de la sainte cène* (Neuchâtel: Delachaux et Niestlé, 1948), passim.

Lietzmann, H., *Messe und Herrenmahl* (Bonn: A. Marcus und E. Weber Verlag, 1926), pp. 249-55.

Sloyan, G. S., " 'Primitive' and 'Pauline' Concepts of the Eucharist," *Catholic Biblical Quarterly,* XXIII (1961), pp. 1-13.

II. *Relationships among the Accounts of Institution*

Benoit, P., "Le récit de la cène dans Lc. XXII, 15-20," *Revue Biblique,* XLVIII (1939), pp. 357-93.

Betz, J., *Die Eucharistie in der Zeit der griechischen Väter,* Vol. I, No. 1 (Freiburg im Br.: Herder, 1955), pp. 1-38; Vol. II, No. 1 (1961), pp. 10-26.

Higgins, A. J. B., *op. cit.*, pp. 24-44.

Jeremias, J., *op. cit.*, passim.

Schürmann, H., *Die Paschamahlbericht Lk 22, (7-14) 15-18* (Münster, Westf.: Aschendorffsche Verlagsbuchhandlung, 1953), passim.

——, *Der Einsetzungszericht Lk 22, 19-20* (Münster, Westf.: Aschendorffsche Verlagsbuchhandlung, 1955), passim.

——, *Der Abendmahlsbericht Lukas 22, 7-38* (Paderborn: Ferdinand Schöningh, 1957), pp. 18-45.

III. Genuineness of Luke 22: 19b-20.

See the references in the previous section and also:

Benoit, P. "Luc. XXII, 19b-20," *Journal of Theological Studies,* XLIX (1948), pp. 145-47.

Kilpatrick, G. D., "Luke XXII, 19b-20," *Journal of Theological Studies,* XLVII (1946), pp. 49-56.

Throckmorton, B. H., "The Longer Reading of Lk 22, 19b-20," *Anglican Theological Review,* XXX (1948), pp. 55-56

IV. Liturgical Character of the Words of Institution

Betz, J., *op. cit.*, Vol. I, No. 1, pp. 4-11.

V. Paul's Claim to a Special Revelation

Neuenzeit, P., *Das Herrenmahl.* Studien zur paulinischen Eucharistieauffassung (Munich: Kösel-Verlag, 1960), pp. 82-88.

VI. Comparative Ages of the Accounts of Institution

Betz, J., *op. cit.*, Vol. I, No. 1, pp. 15-26; Vol. II, No. 1, pp. 10-26.

VII. The Relationship of the Last Supper to a Paschal Meal

Jaubert, A., *La Date de la Cène* (Paris: J. Gabalda, 1957).

Jeremias, J., *Die Abendmahlsworte Jesu,* 3rd ed. (Göttingen: Vandenhoeck & Ruprecht, 1960).

VIII. Passover Feast: Origin and Meaning

De Vaux, R., *Ancient Israel: Its Life and Institutions* (London: Darton, Longman and Todd, 1961), pp. 484-504.

Haag, H., "Ursprung und Sinn der Alttestamentlichen Paschafeier," *Das Opfer der Kirche* (Lucerne: Rex-Verlag, 1954), pp. 17-46.

Segal, J. B., *The Hebrew Passover.* From the Earliest Times to A.D. 70 (London: Oxford University Press, 1963).

IX. Passover Ritual

Roth, C., *The Haggadah* (London: Soncino Press, 1959).

X. *Messianic Implications and Relationship of Last Supper to the Kingdom*

Cooke, B., "Synoptic Presentation of the Eucharist as a Covenant," *Theological Studies*, XXI (1960), pp. 1-44.

IX. *Last Supper as an Acted Prophecy*

Dupont, J., "Ceci est mon corps; ceci est mon sang," *Nouvelle Revue Théologique*, LXXX (1958), pp. 1025-41.

XII. *The Theological Viewpoints of the Antioch-Palestinian and Mark and Matthew Accounts of the Institution*

Betz, J., *op. cit.*, Vol. II, No. 1, pp. 26-35.

XIII. *Meaning of Sōma and Haima (Body and Blood)*

Betz, J., *op. cit.*, Vol. I, No. 1, pp. 38-53.

XIV. *The Origin and Meaning of Diathēkē (Berîth)*

Flanagan, N., "The Covenant and Its Growth," *American Ecclesiastical Review*, CXLIV (1960), pp. 145-56.

Hindley, J. C., "The Meaning and Translation of Covenant," *The Bible Translator*, XIII (1962), pp. 90-101.

Mendenhall, G. F., "Law and Covenant in Israel and the Ancient Near East," *The Biblical Archaeologist*, XVII (1954), pp. 26-76.

XV. *Religious Significance of the Eucharistic Words and Gestures at the Last Supper*

Betz, J., *op. cit.*, passim.

———, "Die Eucharistie als sakramentale Gegenwart des Heilsereignises 'Jesus' nach dem ältesten Abendmahlsbericht," *Geist und Leben*, XXXIII (1960), pp. 166-75.

Dupont, J., *op. cit.*

XVI. *The Use of the Terms "Flesh" and "Blood" to express Union in Ancient Israel*

De Vaux, R., *op. cit.*, pp. 10-11.

Pedersen, J., *Israel: Its Life and Culture I-II* (Oxford: University Press, 1926), pp. 267-68.

XVII. *Significance of Memorial Rite in the Old and New Testament*

Schildenburger, J., "Die Gedächtnischaracter des alt- und neutestamentlichen Pascha," *Opfer Christi und Opfer der Kirche*, ed. B. Neuenheuser (Düsseldorf: Patmos-Verlag, 1960), pp. 75-97.

Thurian, M., *L'Eucharistie*. Mémorial du Seigneur, sacrifice d'action de grâce et d'intercession (Neuchâtel: Delachaux et Niestlé S.A., 1959).

XVIII. Subject of the Remembrance in the Eucharistic Celebration

Jeremias, J., *Die Abendmahlsworte Jesu*, 3rd ed., pp. 229-46.

Kilpatrick, G. D., "L'Eucharistie dans le Nouveau Testament," *Revue de Théologie et de Philosophie*, XCVII (1964), pp. 193-204.

Kosmala, H., "Das tut zu meinen Gëdachtnis, *Novum Testamentum*, IV (1960), pp. 81-94.

CHAPTER THREE

I. Sacramental Realism Predicated of the Eucharist in 1 Corinthians

Neuenzeit, P., *op. cit.*, pp. 175-83, passim.

II. Relationship of the Eucharist to the Church in 1 Corinthians

Best, E., *One Body in Christ*. A Study in the Relationship of the Church to Christ in the Epistles of the Apostle Paul (London: S.P.C.K., 1955), pp. 87-91, passim.

Bornkamm, G., "Herrenmahl und Kirche bei Paulus," *Zeitschrift für Theologie und Kirche*, LIII (1956), pp. 312-49.

Neuenzeit, P., *op. cit.*, pp. 188-219.

Robinson, J. A. T., *The Body*. A Study in Pauline Theology (London: SCM Press, 1955), pp. 56 ff., passim.

CHAPTER FOUR

I. Literary Unity of John 6

Borgen, P., "The Unity of the Discourse in Jn 6," *Zeitschrift für die Neutestamentliche Wissenschaft*, L (1959), pp. 277-78.

———, "Observations on the Midrashic Character of Jn 6," *Zeitschrift für die Neutestamentliche Wissenschaft*, LIV (1963), pp. 232-40.

Ruckstuhl, E., *Die literarische Einheit des Johannesevangelium* (Freiburg in der Schweiz: Paulusverlag, 1951), pp. 220-71.

Schürmann, H., "Jn 6, 51c—ein Schüssel zur grossen johanneischen Brotrede," *Biblische Zeitschrift*, II (1958), pp. 244-62.

———, "Die Eucharistie als Repräsentation und Application des Heilsgeschehens nach Joh. 6, 53-58," *Trierer Theologische Zeitschrift*, LXVIII (1959), pp. 30-45, 108-18.

II. Source of Material

Cerfaux, L., "La section des pains (Mk VI, 31—VIII, 26; Mt XIV, 13—XVI, 12)," *Synoptische Studien Alfred Wikenhauser zum siebszigten Geburtstag dargebracht* (Munich: K. Zink Verlag, 1953), pp. 64-77.

Gärtner, B., *John 6 and the Jewish Passover* (Lund: C. W. K. Gleerup, 1959), pp. 6-13.

III. *Influences on Literary Composition*

Barrett, C. K., "The Old Testament and the Fourth Gospel," *Journal of Theological Studies,* XLVIII (1947), pp. 155-69.

Feuillet, A., "Les thèmes bibliques majeurs du discours sur le pain de vie," *Nouvelle Revue Théologique,* LXXXII (1962), pp. 803-22, 918-1062.

Daube, D., *The New Testament and Rabbinic Judaism* (London: London University Press, 1956), pp. 27-51.

Gärtner, B., *op. cit.,* pp. 14-29.

Gertner, M., "Midrashim in the New Testament," *Journal of Semitic Studies,* VII (1962), pp. 267-92.

Guilding, A., *The Fourth Gospel and Jewish Worship* (Oxford: Clarendon Press, 1960), pp. 58-68.

Kilmartin, E. J., "Liturgical Influences on John 6," *Catholic Biblical Quarterly,* XXII (1960), pp. 183-91.

Ziener, G., "Johannesevangelium und urchristliche Passafeier," *Biblische Zeitschrift,* II (1958), pp. 263-74.

IV. *Polemical Interest in John 6*

Betz, J., *Die Eucharistie in der Zeit der griechischen Väter,* Vol. I, No. 1, pp. 26-35; Vol. II, No. 1, pp. 189-200.

Kilmartin, E. J., "A First Century Chalice Dispute," *Sciences Ecclésiastiques,* XII (1960), pp. 403-8.

V. *History of the Interpretation of John 6: 54-59*

Cavallera, F., "L'interprétation du chapitre VI de saint Jean. Une controverse exégétique au Concile de Trente," *Revue d'Histoire Ecclésiastique,* X (1909), pp. 687-709.

Siedlecki, E. J., *A Patristic Synthesis of John VI, 54-55* (Mundelein, Ill.: Saint Mary of the Lake Seminary, 1956).

VI. *Interpretation of John 6*

Barrett, C. K., *The Gospel According to St. John* (London: S.P.C.K., 1955).

Bultmann, R., *Das Evangelium des Johannes* (Göttingen: Vandenhoeck und Ruprecht, 1950).

Daube, D., *op. cit.*

Dodd, C. H., *The Interpretation of the Fourth Gospel*, 5th ed. (Cambridge: University Press, 1960).

Hoskyns, E. C., *The Fourth Gospel*, 2nd ed. (London: Faber and Faber Ltd., 1947).

Lagrange, M. J., *Évangile selon saint Jean*, 5th ed. (Paris: Librairie Lecoffre, 1936).

Léon-Dufour, X., "Le mystère du pain de vie," *Recherches de Science Religieuse*, XLVI (1958), pp. 481-523.

Mollat, D., "Le chapitre VIe de s. Jean," *Lumière et Vie*, XXXI (1957), pp. 107-19.

Ruckstuhl, E., "Wesen und Kraft der Eucharistie in der Sicht des Johannesevangelium," *Das Opfer der Kirche* (Lucerne: Rex-Verlag, 1954), pp. 48-90.

Stöger, A., *Brot des Lebens* (Munich: Verlag J. Pfeiffer, 1955), pp. 7-88.

VII. A Historical Problem concerning John 6: 54-59

Boismard, M. E., *Du Baptême à Cana* (Paris: Éditions du Cerf, 1956), p. 111, note 25; 141, p. note 10.

Bornkamm, G., "Die Eucharistische Rede im Johannesevangelium," *Zeitschrift für die Neutestamentliche Wissenschaft*, XLVII (1957), pp. 161-69.

Jeremias, J., "Jn 6, 51c-58 redaktionell," *Zeitschrift für die Neutestamentliche Wissenschaft*, XLIV (1952-53), pp. 265-66.

Lagrange, M. J., *op. cit.*, pp. 195-96.

Léon-Dufour, X., *op. cit.*

Schürmann, H., "Eucharistiefeier (urchristliche)," *Lexicon für Theologie und Kirche*, III, 2nd ed. (1959), cols 1159-62.

CHAPTER FIVE

Schürmann, H., "Die Gestalt der urchristlichen Eucharistiefeier," *Münchener Theologische Zeitschrift*, VI (1955), pp. 107-31.

Stöger, A., "Die Eucharistiefeier des Neuen Testamentes," *Eucharistiefeier in der Christenheit*, ed. T. Bogler (Maria Laach: Verlag Ars Liturgica, 1960), pp. 10-19.

CHAPTER SIX

Audet, J. P., "Esquisse historique du genre littéraire de la 'bénédiction' juive et l' 'eucharistie' chrétienne," *Revue Biblique*, LXV (1958), pp. 371-99.

————, *La Didache*. Instruction des Apôtres (Paris: J. Gabalda, 1958), pp. 377-98.

Fraigneau-Julien, B., "Éléments de la structure fondamentale de l'eucharistie. Bénédiction, anamnèse et action de grâces," *Recherches de Science Religieuse*, XXXIV (1960), pp. 35-61.

Gamber, K., "Anklange an das Eucharistiegebet bei Paulus und das jüdische Kiddush," *Ostkirchliche Studien*, IX (1960), pp. 254-64.

CHAPTER SEVEN

Kilmartin, E. J., "The Eucharistic Cup in the Primitive Liturgy," *Catholic Biblical Quarterly*, XXIV (1962), pp. 32-43.

Schürmann, H., "Das apostolische Interesse am eucharistischen Kelch," *Münchener Theologische Zeitschrift*, IV (1953), pp. 223-31.

Index of References